The Author

Kevin J. Swick is Professor of Education, Department of Instruction and Teacher Education at the University of South Carolina, Columbia. He is the author or coauthor of several other NEA publications: *Maintaining Productive Student Behavior, Disruptive Student Behavior in the Classroom, Teacher Renewal, Parenting, Stress and the Classroom Teacher, Parents and Teachers as Discipline Shapers,* and *A Proactive Approach to Discipline: Six Professional Development Modules for Educators.* He also developed the *NEA Training Program on Discipline and Classroom Management.*

The Advisory Panel

Richard S. Greene, Board Certified Medical Psychotherapist; retired Special Education teacher; founder and editor-in-chief, *Exceptional People's Quarterly*, Fresno, California

Robert L. Hamm, Language Arts teacher, West Linn High School, Oregon

John Joyce, Mathematics teacher, Winchester High School, Massachusetts

Margaret Lantz Petrella, Social Studies teacher, Mt. Airy, Maryland

Peter G. Vlachos, Department of General Planning, City and County of Honolulu, Hawaii

Nancy Hager White, first grade teacher, Hamlin Elementary School, West Virginia

STUDENT STRESS:
A Classroom
Management System

Kevin J. Swick

nea **PROFESSIONAL LIBRARY**
National Education Association
Washington, D.C.

Note

The opinions expressed in this publication should not be construed as representing the policy or position of the National Education Association. Materials published as part of the Analysis and Action Series are intended to be discussion documents for teachers who are concerned with specialized interests of the profession.

Library of Congress Cataloging-in-Publication Data

Swick, Kevin J.
  Student stress.

  (Analysis and action series)
  "Produced in cooperation with the NEA Mastery in
Learning Project."
  Bibliography: P.
  1. Classroom management.   2. Stress (Psychology)—
Prevention.   3. Students—United States—Mental health.
I. NEA Mastery in Learning Project.   II. Title.
III. Series.
LB3013.25.S94   1987   371.1'024   87-7051
ISBN 0-8106-1696-3

CONTENTS

Chapter 1
INTRODUCTION

A complex society is a potentially explosive context in which stress (and all of its ramifications) can inhibit the full development of its people. As the "change rate" of a society increases, the intensity and pace of life appear to increase in a similar manner. This can create a dangerous situation, especially if people are ill-prepared and/or have few resources for dealing with the changes. Human beings have a limit to their capacity to enact or respond to life events. When this limit is surpassed, physiological and/or socioemotional signals appear to warn people that they have exceeded available capacity. If these signals, such as psychosomatic illness, physical warnings, or mental fatigue, are ignored, a cycle of negative stress-related problems might result.

The severity of stressors and their impact on social life are examined in a recent report:

> In the past 30 years doctors and health officials have come to realize how heavy a toll stress is taking on the nation's well-being. According to the American Academy of Family Physicians, two-thirds of office visits to family physicians are prompted by stress-related symptoms. (79, p. 48)*

This same report goes on to outline the tragic cost of uncontrolled stress to the total society:

> Based on national samples, these costs have been estimated at $50 billion to $75 billion a year, more than $750 for every U.S. worker. Stress is now known to be a major contributor, either directly or indirectly, to coronary heart disease, cancer, lung ailments, accidental injuries, cirrhosis of the liver and suicide—six of the leading causes of death in the U.S. (79, p. 48)

Beyond the immediate damage that stress has created is the danger that children and young people will internalize ineffective coping strategies used by the adult models available to them (19, 20). The increase in children's mental health problems and the epidemic of teenage suicides might well be symptoms of a society that has fallen prey to an uncontrolled life style. It is clear that an educational plan is essential to promoting ways of controlling stress. This plan must involve all societal institutions if it is to represent some common agreement on how to alter

---

*Numbers in parentheses appearing in the text refer to the Bibliography beginning on page 92.

the current situation. Classroom teachers, as societal leaders, can play a major role in both educating students on how to deal with stress and involving parents and citizens in efforts to provide students with exemplary models of positive stress-management techniques (7).

Two factors that have been related to successful stress management are the acquisition and use of control skills, and the development and use of a systemic process to assess levels of stress and to design implementing stress-management strategies (30, 44). A lack of control skills has been linked to increases in all of the stress symptoms and to a variety of social ailments. Assessments of stressed adults indicate that the response patterns they exhibit were developed early in life and then continuously refined but not drastically altered. These assessments also point out that victims of negative stress are typically unaware of the conditions prompting their stress and lack the skills and strategies necessary to deal with stress (81).

Fifty years of research on stress has produced a viable framework for making stress a functional part of life. The interactions of body-mind and person-environment are more clearly understood than they were in the past. For example, it is now known that the human alarm system reacts to any stress, thus increasing the person's physiological and mental energy levels. When the stress-inducing situation is dealt with or alleviated, human beings return to some form of equilibrium. However, continued intense levels of stress can extend the individual beyond his or her capacity and trigger the body-mind to send signals that it is under attack. Stressors that are perceived to be especially threatening create a flight/fear response. Migraine headaches, heart trouble, ulcers, and liver damage are physical signs that the human system is under extreme pressure that could result in burnout (54).

Learning to control one's responses to stress and planning for positive stress arrangements are techniques that have proved successful in countering potentially harmful situations. Two behaviors that are continually exhibited by effective stress managers are the acquisition of an understanding of stress and how to act on it, and the ability to plan for productive interactions in the environment (47). For example, Anita felt burned out last year and spent time studying why she felt this way. She found that she was involved in too many activities and was creating unnecessary stress for herself. By planning fewer, but more rewarding activities for the next year, she felt sure that she would be more effective. Ned had a different stressor to deal with. While he enjoyed sales work, he did not like the company he worked for; it was an extremely negative situation. By changing his job, Ned was able to continue doing what he liked but in an environment more to his liking.

While a great deal of effort is being directed toward teaching adults

8

how to resolve negative stress, the most encouraging result of stress research is that children and adolescents can also acquire the skills needed to prevent stress-related syndromes (40). Prevention of stress-related problems in students promises not only better academic performance but also, more importantly, healthier human beings. Burned-out children not only do poorly in school but also fall prey to behavior patterns that make them prime candidates for more serious social maladies (19, 20, 21). Studies of adolescent suicide, for example, point out that the suicidal person usually had a history of stress-related maladies and was unable to construct a context for resolving them (56).

The more complex the societal structure, the more guidance children and adolescents need in dealing with life. Today's students are bombarded by multiple messages that require endless choices on their part. Early and continuing educational experiences in dealing with stress can enable students to develop life styles in which choices are made in a mindful way.

Teachers often see the results of student stress in behavioral problems and poor academic performance. Observant teachers report that excessive stress is a major impediment to student learning. Students who are absorbed in the complexities of family problems or other crises usually suffer from a shortage of energy for use in school functioning. Teachers who acquire an understanding of stress and the skills necessary for dealing with it can educate children in methods of stress management. One example of how this process can work is the teacher who responds to student concerns in a supportive manner, helping the student articulate the issue and develop strategies for resolving it (39).

Two additional roles teachers can fill relate to the design of their classrooms (with specific reference to stress) and their influence on the community. The classroom is a potentially stressful context. When teachers become sensitive to the critical dimensions of stress as it can emerge in the classroom setting, they have taken the first step toward turning the classroom into a healthy and growing environment. Learning environments that place the individual in the center of the decision-making process are usually designed to engage students in creative, productive social and educational experiences.

As community leaders, teachers should focus on the adult role in preventing and/or resolving unhealthy stress in the family, school, and neighborhood. Adult and community education efforts might include awareness projects, stress-management workshops, and seminars that bring people together to share ideas on how to manage stress-inducing environments in better ways (9).

Stress is, of course, inherent in the nature of life. The benefit of continued study of stress is that it is revealing that people can harness the energy that would normally be lost as a result of excessive stress and redirect it toward more productive ends. If children and adolescents can acquire a proactive framework for dealing with stress, their adult lives should be more productive than is currently the case (77).

In order for teachers and students to deal effectively with stress, they must understand the three dimensions of time, space, and relationships. These three dimensions provide the context in which all stress-inducing events occur. Both the quantitative and qualitative aspects of these dimensions are possible stressors. They also provide the major clues to the prevention or resolution of negative stress (33).

In and of itself, time is a neutral construct. It is the manner in which it is defined, perceived, and used that makes it a potentially stressful part of life. The way time is used in the classroom, for example, can foster positive learning attitudes or create a sense of fear and rigidity in children. How a teacher uses time sends a message to students about how the learning process is to be carried out. When time is seen as a stressor, the classroom becomes less effective than when it is perceived as a part of the learning process (41). Once the notion that "time controls me" takes hold, time becomes a potentially dangerous source of anxiety. The qualitative aspect of this is that when people find no meaning or negative meaning in their time usage on a continuing basis, their stress level increases (64). A classroom full of bored children is fertile ground for discipline problems.

An individual's physical, social, and psychological space is another source of stress. Physical space that is cramped, rigid, and limited in utility is certain to produce tension and anxiety among the inhabitants. The way in which the classroom setting is defined—that is, how space is used—has much to do with the "stress index" of the students (30). In order for the physical environment to be supportive of productive learning, it must be managed so that students can use all available space in useful ways, pursue learning in an active manner, and participate in adapting it to their learning needs (73).

An individual's sense of personal and social space is also clearly linked to stress-related issues. For example, Byrnes (13) observes that forgotten children (students who go unnoticed in the classroom) appear to have no special place in the school. Knowing that one is a part of the social ecology is essential to mental health and overall cognitive functioning (22).

One of the greatest sources of student stress is a lack of knowledge of how to use the social ecology. Classrooms that facilitate social learning opportunities are more likely to promote students' mental health than are quiescent learning arrangements (14). Using physical, social, and psychological space effectively is a crucial life-management skill. Adults

10

who have a history of poor management behavior in this area are more likely to suffer from stress-related problems (54).

How stressful any environment is can be determined by how people relate to each other in it. The ways people interact with each other create a pattern of relationships that support or impede their individual learning efforts (77). Peer conflicts, poor teacher-child relationships, and a lack of meaningful linkages to the family promote stressful classroom contexts. Environments that lack a positive human relationship dimension tend to stimulate high amounts of stress. Pelletier (64) indicates that stress sources in the work environment include conflict with supervisors, conflict with co-workers, job dissatisfaction, work overload, lack of support, and negative interpersonal relationships. Similar findings have been reported for classroom and school environments. Classrooms in which children are always quiet, few work artifacts are displayed, and human social functions are always kept at a level of formality are certain to create stress. Such contexts produce emotionally malnourished children and inhibit their full learning potential (76).

A systematic approach to managing stress has proved successful; when people learn to anticipate, plan, and carry out strategies that reduce their stress, they enhance their development and learning potential (9). A management system for examining stress and planning for control of stress in various social contexts includes the following components: identification of the major sources of stress, an in-depth analysis of the dimensions of stress in the specific context under study, and a systematic plan for alleviating the stress-inducing elements in the environment. Research findings support the notion of involving students in developing both stress-management skills and a life style that promotes proactive living (64). In addition, classroom management schemes that encourage student involvement, focus on positive interpersonal relationships, encourage the formation of positive self-concepts, and provide time-space arrangements in which individual and group needs can be met have been shown to promote mental health and eliminate negative stress (67).

Chapter 2
SOURCES OF STRESS

The literature on stress is clear on the following points: stress is a subjective response to a particular situation or series of events; it influences the individual's total body-mind system; it is controllable; and it has many sources including personal, social, psychological, and ecological sources (30). There are certain sources of stress that people will experience during their normal development: childhood, adolescence, adulthood, and the aging process. In addition, most people will experience separation anxiety when entering school, moving to a new community, losing a close friend, acquiring a new job, and being involved in many other normal life happenings (6). The "built-in" stressors of modern living, such as noise pollution, traffic jams, and rapid-paced living, are additional factors that influence people. Indeed, many researchers believe that unhealthy levels of stress are a part of our contemporary life style (79). However, researchers also note that individuals control their own behavior, and, thus, the resolution to many stress-related issues lies in increasing people's skill in controlling their involvement in the environment (44).

STRESS IS AN INDIVIDUAL'S RESPONSE TO LIFE

The initial source of stress is an individual's response to a situation or series of events. This response is based on a perception that the stressor is unsettling, anxiety producing, and disruptive to one's usual life pattern. Further, the perception is based on the individual's learning experiences, which have been acquired over the life span (8). Recent research on learning indicates that through a process of "patterning," one develops a perceptual orientation toward the environment and her or his resulting interactions in it (34). Thus, from early learning experiences an individual establishes a framework for viewing the world and, through continual refinement, develops a life style (48). If this framework offers limited ways to assimilate and accommodate new experiences, the probability that this person will develop stress-related problems is quite high. However, an individual who sees new ideas, different experiences, and new learning as exciting and rewarding is usually able to deal with stress in a productive manner (29).

Evidence suggests that high-stress behavior patterns are formed very early in life. For example, Elkind reports that young children who experience the "hurried child" syndrome appear to be establishing a stressed life style that will inhibit their full development:

> Perhaps the most serious implication of this research is that patterns of reaction to stress established in childhood can be carried over into adulthood and become autonomous. Hurried children, for example, may not show serious symptoms in childhood but may carry with them patterns of emotional response that can lead to serious illness as adults. (19, p. 170)

Individuals who tend to be abnormally dependent on events, things, and people external to themselves are more stress ridden than are self-reliant people (48). Consider, for example, the child who is very dependent on others to initiate and implement problem-solving tasks. This child is certain to face new situations with high anxiety, especially when left to his or her own initiative. Erikson's construct that young children need many positive experiences in initiating and resolving socioemotional issues supports the need to develop children's control skills (22, 24).

The importance of well-being in each individual's response to life is clearly seen in the studies on stress. The meeting of basic needs, such as love, trust, nutrition, sleep, and physical health, is essential to human readiness to deal with stress (64). Current stress research substantiates the observation that people who lead deficit-oriented lives appear to be fearful, insecure, and fate filled. For example, children who suffer from poor nutrition, a negative family environment, and poor health are more likely to develop stress symptoms (39).

Before an individual can create a personal framework for using life stress in creative, positive ways, s/he must develop proactive perceptual patterns. Control of one's actions emanates from a belief system. People with a totally negative view of the world and the future are not likely to search for options when dealing with concrete issues, such as work tasks, parenting, or social conflicts with peers. High-stress people have passive, rather rigid behavior patterns (58). Unable to analyze and plan in the face of certain stressors, many individuals (including children and adolescents) resort to defensive, impulsive, and inefficient modes of living (52).

Individuals who exhibit a high degree of control over their ecology usually have access to an important stress-management element: a strong interpersonal support system (44). Studies of stressed children, for example, report that "aloneness" is common among these children. Cut off from parents, teachers, friends, and peers, many children lack the human resources needed for dealing with stress (52). A common scenario is for the child to sense high expectations from parents and teachers, to experience a rapid-paced life style, and to become highly frustrated in attempting to meet expectations without adequate resources or positive ways of dealing with this anxiety (5). Finding one's context to be unsupportive and uncaring is a major reason cited by adolescents for their acquiescence in the face of many stressors (83).

The complexity of society requires that people be rather creative and sophisticated in dealing with the issues of identity, social meaning, job skills, and self-development. Because of the substantiated increases in stress-related diseases and problems, today's students must develop a high locus of internal control. This control can best be fostered by assuring that children have their basic needs met, are provided ample nurturing, become a meaningful part of the family-school-community context, receive educational experience in dealing with stress in proactive modes, and are encouraged to try new approaches to problem solving (37, 38). The alienation exhibited by stressed students can be alleviated by involving them in situations that validate and strengthen their roles in life (10).

A WORLD OF STRESS

The nature of modern life is such that some stress is inherent in everything people undertake. As technology has increased the number of choices people can make, the tendency to choose more than one can handle has emerged as part of the American life style. Changes in the "ecology of living" can be categorized into the following stress areas: technological stress, work stress, family stress, neighborhood-community stress, biosocial stress, and global stress (6, 23, 48). Whether occurring in isolation or in combination, these stress areas are a major source of individual and group problems. Of special importance is the fact that these stressors can have a negative impact on the development and learning of children and adults.

The outcomes and the life processes that have emerged from a century of technological change have created an inherently stressful life style. Individuals are exposed to massive amounts of information, expected to achieve a knowledge level never before experienced in human history, encouraged to adopt a "fast lane" style of functioning, and socialized to consume more than they produce (10, 64). Left uncontrolled, the techno-paced society can seduce people into a life pattern so stimulating that it erodes their power over an extended time period. This cumulative stress affects people differently: some explode periodically, while others experience the damage later in life in the form of ulcers, heart disease, or some other psychobiological diseases (20, 54). The importance of having control over forces in the environment becomes evident when examining who is affected by the technology stress syndrome. People who are skilled in dealing with new ideas and who have a sense of control over their lives are more effective in managing the dynamics of a constantly changing world (44, 49, 79).

Adults identify work-related stress as a major impediment to their full functioning (32). Interestingly, children and adolescents identify school stress as a primary stressor. Work stress has many elements: boredom, excessive demands, low pay, personal conflicts with supervisors, negative influence on family context, health hazards, mental stress, and combinations of these and other such elements (32, 54). Stressors that occur at work or in relation to the work place can impact all aspects of an individual's life. High-technology, low-person-centered work places have been causally related to family problems, health concerns, and the emergence of alienation in adults and in children (32). The humanization of the work environment in terms of flexible schedules, closer relationships to family and community, and more reasonable job expectations is the positive result of worker input on how to create truly productive work places (10, 48). Employer investments in the quality of their employees' lives are a positive step toward reducing the amount of stress generated by the work place. A similar modus operandi is being proposed to make schools less stressful and more appealing (29, 34, 67).

The family is the context in which people attempt to share their stress and rebuild their integrity in order to deal with the external world. Thus, it is no surprise that family stress is the form of anxiety that most people experience (3, 15, 35, 47). The continued rise in family maladies such as child and/or spouse abuse indicates that family burnout is becoming a major social problem (5, 38). The work performance of adults and the school performance of children are negatively influenced by family problems. It appears that families are often overwhelmed by the stress that emerges from external sources as well as from dealing with role changes that are inherent in modern life. Marital conflict, economic problems, parent-child dissonance, and family-neighborhood problems are some of the stress situations families confront. Parents point to a "time-crunch" and a lack of resources as the major stressors families face. Time-management workshops and programs on communication skills have helped families deal with stress (7, 38, 84).

Many families experience additional stressors as a result of their neighborhood or community context. Unsafe communities, for example, contribute to a rise in fear and, in effect, "require" human energy that could be used to promote better living conditions. The deterioration of many neighborhoods has also caused an increase in sociopsychological problems (33, 48). Supportive neighborhoods provide people with resources to combat the stress they experience. For example, the availability of quality day care has been linked to more positive attitudes in parents toward their children and their work places (10). The community can increase people's control of stress through quality educational programs (17, 30).

Whether the result of other stressors or a primary source itself, biosocial stress is evidenced in many of the modern disease syndromes. For example, recent research has established linkages among many allergic reactions and high stress levels in people. Stress has also been related to heart disease, hypertension, ulcers, and other disorders. In some cases the source is a biological deficiency resulting from poor nutrition or other physical sources. In other cases the source may be psychosocial, as with severe depression. In many situations it is biosocial, meaning the causal elements are interrelated. Major improvements have taken place when individuals acquire skills in locating the stressors, receive help in dealing with them, and get involved in altering the conditions that promote the stressors (30, 48, 54).

Children and adults are experiencing an increase in what might be called "global stress." Mass communications have reduced the psychological time and space in which people live. While in past centuries people were at least able to conceptualize a workable future, residents of today's global village often visualize a bleak future. Some social scientists point to world dynamics as one reason adults are less optimistic about the future. Nuclear power, global pollution, and regional wars have become a part of being alive. Mental health professionals indicate that children's fear of nuclear holocaust is now a key stressor in their lives. Left unchecked, this fear can be translated into other anxiety-related behaviors. One successful strategy for dealing with this "universal stress" is to involve people in actions that can influence things for the better (33, 64, 68).

It is evident that to be alive in modern times is to experience stress. Research on the ecology of human living indicates that people, given different circumstances and varying levels of skills, see stress in different ways. For example, adults tend to define stress in relation to specific events or patterns of events. Children are more likely to relate stress to anticipated situations or to contexts that are unclear, confusing, or too demanding (30). It is important to understand how and what people see as stressful because the resolution of chronic or cumulative stress is dependent on the individual's ability to gain control over the stressors (or control over how he or she reacts to them), and the longer a person identifies with stressors in negative, fearful modes, the more difficult it is to alter the context (30, 58, 65).

16

ADULT-PERCEIVED STRESS

The difference between adult and child stress is exemplified by the case of the unemployed parent. To the parent it is a specific situation (loss of job and income) that is stressful. To the child it is not unemployment that is cause for concern; rather, it is what unemployment does to the parent and what it does to her or his anticipated future that is alarming (6, 23). Adults identify the following specific stressors as devastating: loss of spouse, loss of job, marital disintegration, major health problems, natural disasters such as flood, and loss of a child or close friend. Stress patterns that adults cite as negatively influencing their lives are continual hurrying, persistent interpersonal conflicts, ongoing financial problems, a chronic sense of being overwhelmed, continued lack of support, and a pervasive feeling of loneliness (30, 32, 48, 64).

Adults form their perceptions of what is stressful over their entire life span. Evidence suggests that early experience, bolstered by continuing educational situations, can influence a person to see events as either challenging or stressful. Clearly, certain happenings such as death or a catastrophe are stressful to everyone. Yet, research suggests that some people have developed positive ways of seeing and dealing with even the most traumatic situation. An analysis of adults who exhibit highly productive modes of dealing with stress reveals that they have developed a great deal of internal control over their life context. This sense of control enables them to sort out events in a meaningful way, to anticipate certain stressors, and to plan creative ways of using stress to their own advantage (32, 42, 49, 64).

Since children copy adult ways of doing things, an understanding of adult-perceived stress is integral to planning programs that will help children respond to stress in positive ways. Children tend to internalize the stress experienced by their parents. What is even more critical is that children tend to adopt the coping strategies their parents use, and they seem to internalize the same perceptual orientation that has served their parents—whether in a positive or a negative way. Thus, an unintended cycle of stress can emerge unless some intervening steps are taken to alter the process (3, 6, 20, 27).

CHILD-PERCEIVED STRESS

Children experience stress as a very concrete process. Most of the stress experienced by young children relates to a sense of powerlessness. This sense of powerlessness occurs in all children at some point, such as when they experience separation from their parents. However, this normal sense of anxiety, while temporarily stressful, is not damaging to children. Research indicates that it is the continuing stress that emerges from children's regular encounters with contexts in which they feel powerless that damages their self-image (19, 20, 21).

Two adult-imposed situations appear to be at the center of stress as it is experienced by children (5, 10, 19, 51). One situation is that in which children are constantly expected to perform roles for which they are not developmentally ready. For example, the child who is continually expected to look after himself or herself for long periods of time is likely to develop severe anxiety about situations that he or she is unable to conceptualize. A second situation exists when children are emotionally overloaded by adult concerns and adult life styles. It is common, for example, for many children to spend the entire day in places away from the primary unit of the family.

Research has identified many of the common sources of stress in children: developmental delays (which place children at a disadvantage in the home, school, and community), sex (boys are more stress prone than girls), developmental stage of life (young children are stressed most by ecological imbalance, while older children are most fearful of specific items such as tests), dysfunctional and/or stress-inducing environments, poverty, illness, hospitalization, disasters, family problems, peer conflicts, and school-related stressors (37, 38).

While most adults have at least some means of coping with stress, children are very dependent on the role models available in their environment. Lacking stress-management skills, many children develop such behavioral responses as constant aggression, sullen and defiant behavior, continual crying, taking pride in antisocial acts, an inability to carry out sustained activity, acting dull and unresponsive, excessive nervousness, hyperactivity, and extreme withdrawal (38). Children who experience continued negative stress are more likely to have major health problems and continued anxiety with social situations such as school (15, 27). Stressed children also seem to be more prone to high anxiety and to acquire a fate-filled perception of life (19, 20).

Children who deal effectively with stress have five key qualities: social competence, problem-solving skills, self-confidence, independence, and an achievement orientation (19). These qualities seem to emerge in children who have productive family environments, access to creative problem solving, and security and continuity in their life space (38). Erikson's construct that children need to develop trust in their surroundings before initiative and autonomy can evolve is certainly substantiated by the research on stress in children (24, 35, 39). The physical, psychological, and social stresses experienced by many children deter them from developing a trusting, inquisitive, and optimistic orientation to life. An

18

ecology that includes space, time, and resources for children to use in building a strong sense of self and a positive relationship with others is the best preventive medicine for stress (5, 9, 38).

READINESS FOR DEALING WITH STRESS

Dealing with stress is much like handling any learning experience; the more one is cognizant of the elements existent in the situation, the more likely it is that the person can handle it. Further, the larger the experiential repertoire is, the greater the chance is that an individual can transfer her or his knowledge and skills to new problems. In a similar sense, an individual who has limited skills for dealing with stress is likely to experience many unnecessary frustrations. Thus, it is not surprising that the person who is ill prepared to deal with stress has the most intense response to it (25, 29, 34).

Three types of readiness need to be considered when dealing with an individual's potential for handling a stressful situation: developmental readiness, cognitive readiness, and psychosocial readiness (7, 20, 23, 60).

Developmental readiness is related to a person's physiological status in terms of health, rest, diet, and so. For example, an individual who is rested, in good health, and physically active is better prepared to deal with stress than is someone who is extremely tired and has a poor diet. Many stressed students who appear to be discipline problems are really sending signals that their physiological needs are being poorly met (37, 41, 45, 54). Another aspect of this readiness area is the life stage (infancy, childhood, adolescence, or adulthood) of the individual. To expect a young child to act like an adult is to invite trouble and is certain to create stress in the child. Elkind (19, 20, 21) has detailed the many inappropriate expectations adults often have of children. For example, placing children in romantic situations for which they are not developmentally ready will clearly cause stress. Unrealistic social and academic expectations on the part of teachers and parents is a major cause of stress and, thus, discipline problems, particularly when children and adolescents are provided little emotional support to handle these contexts (10, 31, 55). One key to limiting the negative stress children and adolescents experience is to make sure that they are physically sound and involved in activities appropriate for their life stage.

Studies of stress reactions indicate that cognitive readiness does increase an individual's ability to deal with problems (9, 75). The simple act of involving a person in choice making reduces stress and increases her or his interest in the situation (44). Knowing how different social contexts work reduces the time and energy needed for adapting to new

19

situations. For example, introducing students to new curricula or discipline elements in advance of their involvement increases their awareness of what will be expected when the new programs are implemented. The ability to respond to new situations is yet another cognitive skill that can reduce stress. Cognitive readiness enables students to anticipate stressors, examine problems rationally, and use creative strategies to resolve problems. While cognitive readiness does not preclude stress, it does give people the skills to control their involvement in stress (7, 28, 29, 40).

An individual's affective orientation toward self, others, and various life contexts is a major influence on how stress is handled. Langer (44), for example, has found that low self-concept is connected to a person's ability to solve problems. Purkey and Novak (67) report that children with low self-esteem seem to be more easily frustrated and prone to respond in stressful ways. Perceptions of significant others also influence the way people relate to difficult circumstances. For example, students' dislike of certain teachers may increase their proclivity toward disruptive behavior. For a variety of reasons, people develop negative feelings about specific places. School anxiety has been linked to such a fear, and resolving that phobia or fear is critical to helping students construct more positive attitudes toward school (8, 21, 22, 41).

Individuals who are physically sound, intellectually skilled, and psychologically secure are likely to deal with most stress in a productive manner. While many stressors are of an ecological nature, many stress-prone individuals appear to increase their "risk" by entering into situations for which they are unprepared.

IDENTITY ANXIETY: TODAY'S MAJOR STRESS

Social scientists appear to agree that modern stress is most intense in terms of developing a secure identity. While people may "see" the work place, school, or family as a major source of stress, it is likely that most people are really expressing their frustration over being unable to define themselves as valid and meaningful parts of the world (22, 23, 24). This identity anxiety surfaces in suicide, disruptive behavior, sullenness, apathy, hyperactivity, and a myriad of other syndromes.

People with little identity—that is, individuals who do not see themselves as special and as critically needed in the world—are usually characterized by some common deficits. One of these deficits is a lack of multiple nurturing experiences. A cold, hostile, and mechanistic ecology is sure to produce an anxiety-ridden child. Another deficit appears to exist in their lack of adult guidance and support. A strong identity is possible only when people have role models they can learn from. Finally,

20

anxiety-ridden people have a history of experiencing life in a fate-filled manner. Lacking in support and guidance, many children and adolescents fail to develop the skills for meaningful interpersonal involvement (27, 37).

People can and have developed healthy identities. Strong support systems, caring environments, and socioeducational designs that empower people to interact in productive ways are keys to having a healthy citizenry. It is clear that a major task is to create families, schools, and communities that value people. The healthy people who are the result of such an ecology will then have the skills to transform stressors into growth experiences (59, 61).

Chapter 3
STRESS IN SCHOOLS AND CLASSROOMS

Stress in any context influences all of the settings connected to it. A child who is hyperactive at home does not alter his or her behavior drastically when entering other environments. The indicators of human stress, such as crime and mental illness, that occur in the community are also evident in the schools. Excessive stress presents a special problem for teachers and students because it impedes the teaching-learning process. Not only does stress have a negative influence on an individual's physiology but also it tends to create a high level of sociopsychological anxiety in groups (2, 3, 11, 34). For example, it has been documented that disruptive and aggressive school behavior patterns increase the anxiety level of everyone in the school. In effect, a pattern of high stress in schools can create a school burnout cycle in which all the participants spend their energy on issues related to fear.

There is a normal range of stress in any school or classroom. Tasks must be completed, new information acquired, and various skills applied to new problems. It is the unhealthy level of stress that has the potential to erode the integrity of the educational program. School and classroom stress emanates from within the school context and from the sources of functioning that the participants bring with them to school (47, 48). Students, teachers, and other school staff often bring in the psychological stress that is a part of their lives outside the school. For example, a child may be under a great deal of stress at home because of her or his parents' marital problems. In such cases the child is negatively influenced by the home situation, usually performs erratically in school, and can negatively influence the behavior of others (35). Teachers who are suffering from excessive stress as a result of personal or financial problems do not usually leave their personal lives at home. In fact, evidence suggests that a teacher's personal life-orientation is a major influence on the social and psychological makeup of the classroom (2, 78).

Within school and classroom settings there are many potential causes of stress: teacher behavior, classroom organization, curriculum focus, student relationships, program philosophy, discipline code, and parent-citizen involvement (3, 21, 55). It is natural for some stress to evolve from school and classroom actions. Excessive stress that pervades the school ecology, however, is damaging not only to students and teachers but also to the total community.

DIMENSIONS OF SCHOOL STRESS

Research has revealed three dimensions of school stress that cause most of the problems related to student and teacher behavior: time, space, and human relations.

Time

Time can be a major source of school stress. The quantitative and the qualitative elements of time influence the ways in which people behave. Both these elements exist in all human interactions and influence those interactions in various ways. For example, the amount of time that we spend on an activity or the amount of time that we are given to complete an activity is very revealing of our value structure. The pace at which we do things also influences our behavior and may affect our value orientation (33). How we use time is the qualitative aspect of this dimension of stress. Sleeping, eating, working, and playing are, in effect, qualities of life that help to define who people are and, in some sense, set a direction for their future. When people ask about the quality of an experience, they are asking about how time is used in relation to the individual's perceived well-being. In this sense any school activity can be viewed as high quality or low quality depending on how the participants perceive it. Thus, the quantitative and qualitative elements of time are major sources of school stress (19, 37, 55, 59).

Common quantitative time stressors identified by students and teachers include rigid schedules, poorly organized schedules, inadequate time frames, and too little time for transition activities (2, 73, 78). Research indicates that when time is seen as rigidly controlling one's behavior, it becomes a negative stressor and impedes human functioning. Thus, a major problem in many schools is that teachers and students see the school day as something to "get through" as opposed to seeing it as a source of learning. Another time stressor cited by school inhabitants is the poor organization of schedules. Just as time can be too tightly planned, it can also be left too open. Poor scheduling can lead to student confusion over what is to be done when and where. Chaos can result, and unnecessary stress is certain to accompany such predicaments (39, 46, 73).

Two factors that students identify as very stressful are these: (1) having too little time to achieve certain tasks, and (2) not having enough time to make the shift to new activities. In sessions with school counselors, students express their frustration over not having enough time to complete schoolwork. Students and teachers sense the stress of "crunched time" and often exhibit their frustration in nonproductive behavior such as high absenteeism and uncooperative attitudes (21, 67, 73). It is true that some anxiety related to time frames results from the fact that participants have poor time-management skills. Yet, the quantitative time element is still a source of stress that must be addressed.

Qualitative elements of time that are identified as major sources of school stress include lack of input on what school time is used for, too much time wasted on meaningless rituals, school activities that often have little to do with real learning, and too much time spent on testing (19, 37, 55, 66). Depending on the school context, many students express clear dissatisfaction with how school time is used. For example, even in good schools, students complain that most of the day is spent on impersonal tasks that add little to their learning and development. Some teachers sense this same stress and point to class size and administrative directives as primary causes of this problem (73, 82). Children and adolescents have a strong desire to learn about themselves and their environment. When this desire is left unattended, it negatively influences the students' total learning system. The "cipher in the classroom" is becoming more prevalent and might signal a need for schools to renew their commitment to personalized education (12, 13, 22).

The tendency in impersonal ecologies is to overprogram time with fairly homogeneous tasks. Student complaints that they rarely have input into how time is used are substantiated by studies of school climate. In far too many cases the program is totally adult directed. In schools in which students are given a significant role in determining the content of the day, stress is reduced and pride in the school increases (21, 28, 29, 53, 67). One of the major stress-reduction skills is controlling self-environment contexts in productive ways. Thus, school leaders should provide students with time-management experiences through which they can strengthen their planning skills (29, 44).

While rituals can be useful in creating school pride, many students and teachers feel stressed by the number of meaningless rituals. Each school should examine such practices as assemblies, daily announcements, and cafeteria policies to determine the extent to which they meet—or fail to meet—student and teacher needs. For example, one ritual—testing—is clearly abused in many schools. Many tests are used for punishment, teacher convenience, or academic appearances. However, when rituals such as testing are appropriately used as a part of the instructional process, they can actually increase student skills. When a significant number of students and teachers perceives the content of schooling as dysfunctional, the stage is set for high stress and poor behavior (39, 48, 55, 73).

Space

School stress is also related to the physical, psychological, and social space of the teaching-learning process. Schools that lack adequate physical space, are unsafe, lack aesthetic appeal, and are not designed to accommodate individual needs are very stressful (38, 47). The physical design of the school should provide students with many opportunities to develop and learn. It should be an "inviting" place; students, teachers, and citizens should feel a sense of personal pride in what takes place there (68).

A psychological sense of space is also critical to productive school behavior. Students and teachers who feel isolated from the school's programs are not only potential stress victims but also potential dropouts. Schools that are rigid in handling "people issues" tend to promote negative stress. When students have the opportunity to define at least part of the school context, they are able to eliminate many stressors and acquire skills in stress management (28, 40).

Human Relations

Significant learning about how to manage stress should take place in the social space in which teaching and learning occur. The existence of student councils, drama clubs, peer teams, informal social events, and other planned social outlets gives evidence of some validity to the construct that learning is enhanced through socialization arrangements. It is through contacts with others (peers, teachers, counselors, etc.) that students acquire feedback on how to respond appropriately to different learning situations. The opportunity to learn from each other is essential for healthy development in people and is a major strategy for preventing or resolving many stress-related issues (9, 14, 40, 53, 59). Environments that allow little self-development, discourage human teaming, and foster a sense of fear in people are certain to be filled with stress (37, 76).

Assessments of school ecologies identify the affective dimension as symbolic of the school's philosophy. The action philosophy of a school is evident in teacher attitudes, student perceptions, parent-citizen support, and actual day-to-day transactions. Schools in which students are viewed as incapable, negative, and unruly promote psychosocial stress. People who believe in and respect one another provide themselves with a human relations framework that precludes many stressors. Schools are usually healthy and positive places in which to teach and learn when humor, sensitivity, empathy, constructive problem solving, and mutual support are a part of the environment (33, 40, 61).

DIMENSIONS OF CLASSROOM STRESS

Classroom stress is an extension of school stress; it is influenced by and is a potential contributor to school stress. On the other hand, it is in the classroom that teachers can have a major impact on stress-related concerns. It is true that for many students their major stressors exist outside the classroom; yet, research indicates that classrooms can also induce a great deal of stress (18, 55, 73). For example, it has been shown that classrooms in which there is an excessive amount of disruptive behavior are also characterized by high levels of stress (67, 77). The design and management of time, space, and human relations can promote stress or act as a preventive force.

Time

The way in which time is organized and used can be called the "time press" of the classroom. In other words, the method in which time is used creates a framework for what can and cannot happen in the classroom. For example, if the entire class period is used for lecture, many student questions will go unanswered, creating needless anxiety over the meaning of various aspects of the content. Another time-related problem occurs when teachers try to cover too much material in a very short period. Such a predicament can cause anxiety in both teachers and students. When the classroom time schedule is too rigid and filled with events that are of little value to the students, boredom often results. Key indicators of poor time usage include too many mechanical learning routines, an over-reliance on teacher-dominated activities, and too many extended large-group sessions. When time is used ineffectively, the likelihood of negative stress increases, and the amount of time students have to explore and develop their natural capacities is limited (5, 33, 39).

An understanding of how time and human learning/development interface is essential to promoting a sound instructional program. Children and adolescents experience time as a natural part of learning and use it to extend and refine their personal development. Mechanistic-quantitative time schemes do not allow for the exploration that is inherent in all meaningful learning (34). When students are able to participate in shaping the time frame for learning, they are less likely to perceive this element of school as stressful.

When time is viewed as a resource, teachers involve students in planning how to use it to meet individual as well as group needs. It is no surprise that Miss James is not bothered because William is spending so much time on his painting of Lake Canton. She does not expect students to use time in a homogeneous manner. Her point is this: students must learn to "plan" their use of time to meet their needs as well as their responsibilities. Thus, part of the day is set aside for choice making and part for meeting needs common to all students.

Langer's work (44) on developing control-building skills in people confirms Miss James's viewpoint on time usage. Individuals who have no choice in shaping their involvement in various contexts experience frustration and impotence, and react in passive or aggressive ways. The potential for negative stress (and resulting discipline problems) increases as the students' involvement in managing time usage decreases (33, 44). One way to apply this idea to the teaching situation is to look at the daily schedule in relation to the "time-management" plan. For example, does the teacher make all the decisions regarding how time is used? Is time always "slotted" for accomplishing teacher-defined tasks? Time is something to be shared among all the participants in the classroom. Involving children and ourselves in planning daily schedules together can strengthen everyone's decision-making skills and ultimately result in a program that uncovers many hidden talents (10, 14, 61).

A related time element is what we do with students: How do we spend class time? Are we doing some activities too often, without a real purpose, or in a rather debunking fashion? Testing is one such practice that often ends up becoming a source of irritation as opposed to a useful learning tool. Excessive testing, unfair assessment practices, and inappropriate use of test/assessment results are clear stressors to students and teachers alike. Another practice that deserves attention is the overuse of teacher-talk. Diversifying time usage through peer-group learning, student-initiated actions, and project-oriented practices has been related to meaningful, cooperative instructional schemes (14, 53, 55, 77).

Time is experienced individually, culturally, and within a developmental framework. Clearly, no classroom management scheme could or should achieve a perfect relationship among these variables. Yet, it is equally obvious that some consonance must exist among individual body time, cultural time, time as dictated by one's stage of development, and classroom time (33). Teachers who become aware of student-time orientation (through observation of behavior and recognition of personal habits) can prevent high levels of stress. An example of poor time pacing exists when young children are expected to function in the same manner as older children. Naturally, in such cases the children who cannot meet the time expectations of the teacher will feel inadequate. Pacing time according to the unique needs of students not only reduces stress but also increases the potential for student talents to emerge in a productive fashion (19, 20, 33, 76).

27

Space

Space is another constant in the classroom context. Research indicates that space usage can either stimulate or impede learning. The "space press" of the classroom has three elements: physical, psychological, and social space (33, 48). Too little physical space or inappropriate use of available space creates the potential for stress. Expecting children to function in adult-size furniture, for example, is certain to spawn problems. Crowding adolescents into rigid and small environments can exaggerate behavior problems that might be more manageable in a functional setting. If students have a sense of impotence in their physical surroundings, stress-related actions such as shoving and pushing are likely to occur (29, 40, 67).

To create a positive "space press," the physical environment should be arranged so that enough space exists for students to pursue active learning, students can use the space in meaningful ways, students can modify the space to suit their learning thrusts, and students feel a sense of responsibility for taking care of their environment (61).

Flexible, but ordered space allows students and teachers to manage their actions in productive ways, thus decreasing the potential for unhealthy stress. It is important that productive space be "incomplete." Children and adolescents are highly active and physically oriented toward constructing things and filling space with the representations of their ideas (34). Space that is filled with adult-developed materials is unlikely to encourage students to develop their talents. Involving students in shaping their space, in taking responsibility for maintaining the physical setting, and in acquiring skills for using space effectively are positive means of preventing stress in the classroom (33, 39, 77).

The most critical aspect of space is the psychological space that students sense as they define themselves as successful, growing learners (10, 33). Research indicates that students who see themselves as "participants" in the classroom ecology acquire the self-confidence they need to become autonomous decision makers (44, 54). A positive "psychological press" exists in classrooms in which children and adolescents are treated as unique individuals and the learning design centers around supporting each student's interests and talents. The following questions will help guide teachers in examining the psychological context of their classrooms:

1. Are students known and respected? That is, do students feel that they are a significant part of the classroom context?

2. Do students feel at ease in questioning what happens in the classroom environment? Indeed, are students encouraged to express their opinions in various ways?

3. Do students see their work displayed and shared with others? Are students involved in a variety of activities through which to develop their individual strengths? (31, 53, 66)

Students develop a sense of fright and flight when they feel closed in or overwhelmed. Students under such stress direct their energy toward escaping or transforming the situation, and, thus, they reduce their constructive participation in classroom learning.

Studies of classroom ecologies indicate that students experience extreme psychological stress when the following conditions occur on a continuing basis: the personal dimension of learning is neglected, student differences are not accommodated, rigid student expectations are enforced without regard to students' developmental and cultural traits, few opportunities exist for student input in the classroom design, and hostile and negative attitudes are prevalent in the classroom (76). Rigidly defined classroom systems do not promote the psychological health of students or teachers, whereas flexibility, sensitivity, and viability make for positive mental health (8, 48, 61).

Studies reveal that students and teachers want the following in their psychological space: a sense of security, a structure that allows for self-growth, meaningful contacts with others, validation that one is important to the functioning of the group, and room to diverge from the group when necessary to carry out new ideas (22, 23, 24). Thus, in planning the physical and/or social arrangement of the classroom, teachers must always return to this question: What does this arrangement do to the individual's sense of psychological space? For example, do teacher and students have a place in the classroom to pursue their individual talents? The planning of psychological space should focus on the following: respecting and nurturing each person's individuality, accepting and valuing each individual's ideas, encouraging student inquiry, fostering student expressiveness and exploration, and integrating various student cultural orientations into the instructional program (10, 22, 67).

Social space provides teachers and students with an arena in which to expand and refine their individuality as well as to build group identity (8, 23). Through social interchange, students not only acquire group functioning skills but also learn how to use their environment as a learning resource. The use of positive instructional strategies such as peer learning teams, group problem-solving tasks, friendship networks, and related social-learning approaches will help students achieve social competence (14, 75, 77).

Classrooms that confine the social development of children and adolescents to adult-defined parameters are certain to dull inquisitive minds and foster unhealthy stress (19, 20). A good mix of guidance and freedom allows children and adolescents to explore the environment in a natural manner. Following are some important questions regarding the social space of the classroom:

1. Are students encouraged to use each other and the teacher as resources for learning?
2. Are students encouraged to resolve their differences through mutual planning?
3. Are students involved in leadership development experiences?
4. Are students involved in taking care of the classroom?
5. Are special achievements and special events recognized through classroom rituals?

Aggression, hostility, and passive behavior patterns are likely to surface in contexts that restrict free social interchange among the participants (77). Children and adolescents have a strong natural proclivity to relate to others, and when this is impeded, unnecessary stress is created (76).

Well-designed classrooms encourage students to create a meaningful social context. Through involvement in informal work areas and in social and recreational outlets, as well as in the formal instructional program, students can be stimulated to learn about each other and how to support each other in their personal and social development (24). Students (as well as teachers and parents) must have access to each other; they must be able to share their thoughts, ask questions, and learn to deal with their disagreements in positive ways. The goal in designing classroom space is not to have the teacher control it but rather to involve students in shaping it so that they can become effective in controlling their lives. As students see their artifacts exhibited and their ideas integrated into the classroom ecology, they will acquire self-confidence and expand their perceptions of their potential to relate to varying situations in harmonious ways (77).

Human Relations

How people relate to one another in various contexts can be called the "human relationship press." In other words, the way people treat each other creates a pattern of relationships that supports or impedes their individual learning efforts (77). It is through human transactions that ideas are shared and products developed and refined.

Positive human relationships strengthen the learning environment by creating a high trust level among students and teachers. When students take an interest in each other's accomplishments and sense a positive group ethos, stress is rarely a problem. A positive "human relationship

30

press" includes actions such as caring, sharing, exhibiting sensitivity, showing respect, extending courtesy, expressing concern, and generally behaving in ways that support productive social learning. Classrooms in which human relationships are rarely nurtured suffer from emotional malnutrition. It is impossible for students to learn how to deal with themselves and others in positive ways when the daily program leaves little or no time for such activities (84).

Teacher actions that promote positive human interactions among students are the most valuable of any teaching behaviors (77). Such behavior is exhibited by the teacher who "plans" for the time and space necessary for students to practice human relationship skills; instructional time is planned with the notion that children will help each other, and learning centers are designed to encourage human interaction. Another example is the teacher who takes time each day to interact with students about topics of concern to them. Classroom arrangements that promote caring are certain to stimulate a healthy stress in students and to influence their social and moral development in positive ways. Some questions to guide assessment of the human relationship context of the classroom are as follows:

1. Take stock of your relationships with students and other staff members. Are you responsive to student interests, concerns, and ideas? Do you consider the needs of other staff in your professional decisions?

2. Examine how you use the time and space facets of the curriculum. Is time so tightly scheduled that students' feelings are never dealt with? Is the psychological climate of the classroom conducive to warm, positive relationships?

3. Are parents encouraged to develop supportive and mutually rewarding relationships with their children? Are parents invited to visit the classroom and participate in the program?

In positive classroom settings, students, parents, and teachers develop respect for each other and internalize constructive ways of relating and responding to their individual and common concerns. The management of time, space, and human relationships in a manner that promotes the unique and active involvement of every student is the basic goal of quality educational programs. It is through interpersonal validation, active participation, and harmonious relationships that students acquire the foundation for becoming lifelong learners. Therefore, teachers who allow time and make room for children and adolescents to undertake their personal learning journey are certain to influence these students in invaluable ways.

31

THE IMPACT OF CLASSROOM STRESS

While most researchers have focused on its negative aspects, stress does have some positive features. Without stress, it would be impossible to learn or to reach for new levels of functioning. The keys to using stress in a productive fashion and to designing situations that prompt healthy stress in students are a knowledge of how individuals function and an understanding of an effective classroom setting.

In the proper context, stress can have a positive impact on student behavior (7, 29). A good example of healthy stress in students occurs when they are motivated to solve problems that are of inherent interest to them. Mr. Johnson has students examine environmental issues by carrying out research in the community. He helps them get started but allows them plenty of latitude to explore issues from many different viewpoints. In art class Miss Rankin involves students in creating collages for a local exhibition in a nearby shopping mall. Projects such as these prompt healthy stress and provide positive directions for student talents.

Healthy stress that emerges within positive, supportive classrooms has many useful outcomes: it tends to increase student motivation to learn, it strengthens student morale, it offers students opportunities to expand their problem-solving skills, it tends to decrease student behavior problems, and it strengthens skills the students need to manage their personal lives (10, 14, 19).

Good teachers support students as they learn how to use stressors in creative, positive ways (7, 77). When students learn how to turn negative situations into learning experiences, they have acquired an invaluable stress-management strategy. For example, Mr. Hayes has been helping John, a fifth grader, develop better study habits. He has helped John plan his weekly work better and, thus, has reduced John's anxiety over being late with assignments. Mrs. Balboni has been working with many of her third grade students on identifying the positive aspects of their behavior. She says, "It has helped them to at least focus on some of the positive aspects of life." Research supports her efforts in that positive self-image and proactive social interaction are related to productive student behavior (77, 78).

A classroom orientation toward positive stress usage also has a constructive impact on teacher behavior (78). When teachers and students are involved in meaningful instructional activities, teachers tend to improve their pedagogical style. When teachers are encouraged to experiment and develop their unique teaching talents, a positive stress is produced in which many creative ideas can be explored. Teacher-child interactions, relationships with peers, parental contacts, and instructional planning are improved when the stress orientation of the classroom is positive (2, 78).

Teacher efforts to resolve negative stress situations in the classroom can result in positive happenings. For example, it is known that teachers who successfully resolve discipline problems tend to gain self-confidence and improve their classroom control skills. Additional examples of how teachers can use challenging situations to create positive outcomes in the classroom and in their professional efforts include the following: designing flexible learning arrangements and, thus, maximizing available resources; improving classroom management skills through continued professional development experiences; maintaining regular contacts with parents; engaging in personal renewal activities such as time-management programs; and setting aside regular class time for interacting with students on issues of concern to them (18, 32, 47, 78).

When negative stress is pervasive and continuous, it can have a devastating impact on all concerned. When people perceive stressors as potentially harmful and see themselves as unable to alter the situation, a damaging outcome is likely. If negative stress continues unabated, an individual's total system is negatively influenced. In some cases the damage may not surface until later, but in many cases it manifests itself almost immediately in a variety of ways (6, 12, 19). Researchers have documented that stress can erode the physical, psychological, cognitive, and socioemotional fabric of people (37, 38).

Children under heavy stress suffer from various problems: ill feelings, distorted cognition, antisocial actions, and physiological dysfunction. Blom, Cheney, and Snoddy (7) cite the following common stress reactions among children: constant crying, extreme withdrawal, excessive fighting, drastic mood shifts, unusual depression, poor achievement, failure to complete simple tasks, constant tardiness, truancy, impulsiveness, hyperactivity, physical sickness, and constant daydreaming. It is natural for all children to respond to occasional stress in such ways, but when these responses characterize a child's pattern of daily functioning, they signal a serious disruption in her or his system.

Elkind (19) proposes that the "hidden impact" of stress may be more serious than the symptomatic responses. When children suffer from high levels of any type of stress (positive or negative), their ability to perform with any consistency will eventually be eroded. Constant disruption of the child's homeostasis creates an erratic pattern of "highs and lows" that makes it difficult to learn and develop in productive ways (39). The consonance that provides the child with a framework for internalizing reasoned responses to life situations is destroyed when the child experiences constant disruptions. Thus, a major result of stress can be the destruction of the child's life system. Without such a system for responding to life, the child is confronted with constant confusion, develops poor social and cognitive behaviors, usually loses self-confidence, and experiences many difficulties functioning in the classroom (29, 44, 68).

Stressed children experience more failure, have difficulties with peers, tend to withdraw from challenge, and are likely to face future social problems unless they gain control of their situation (29, 52). The destruction of self-confidence is the "core" result of childhood stress. It can occur quietly, going unnoticed by others, or it can surface in periodic outbursts of anger. Either way, the child acquires a sense of helplessness that prompts a cycle of unproductive behavior that can delimit the potential of his or her life (19, 23, 24, 25).

Classroom teachers are especially vulnerable to the negative facets of stress. In many respects teachers are the receivers of multiple stressors passed to them by children, parents, peers, and personal friends. Swick and Hanley (78) explicate the major indicators of stressed teachers: constant irritability, excessive absenteeism, poor work performance, unusual social withdrawal, negative perceptions of students, poor human relationships, and low self-image. Teachers functioning in "stressed classrooms"—in which space is minimal, resources limited, class size large, and student-related problems excessive—are likely to confront many direct challenges to their self-confidence. Alschuler (2), for example, describes the "burnout cycle" that many teachers experience as symptomatic of the serious problems that exist in many classrooms.

A continuous erosion of control skills in teachers is a clear result of stress. Energy is misdirected toward the anxiety experienced as a result of various problems, and many necessary management practices are neglected. The cycle can continue to unfold as the poorly managed classroom creates even more stress and raises teacher anxiety to even higher levels. As actual control skills deteriorate, perceived mastery related to interactions in the environment is also negatively influenced (29, 44).

Teacher interactions with students are dramatically altered under high levels of stress. While "healthy" teachers tend to respond to student questions in a positive manner and relate to their concerns empathetically, stressed teachers tend to react defensively and often create a psychological wall around themselves. When teachers perceive students in negative ways, there is less interaction between them, and the contacts that do occur are usually punitive, authoritarian, and/or impersonal (51, 55, 67). Cycles of negative interpersonal student-teacher relationships are certain to create more stress in the classroom until a proactive approach to controlling stress and promoting an effective set of teacher behaviors is taken (77, 78).

A loss of optimism about future events is certainly a dangerous situation because people function in relation to their projections of future possibilities. Teachers functioning under high levels of stress have a bleak outlook about the future. They tend to be cynical, pessimistic, and isolated from actions that might produce positive outcomes. In many cases this poor future image becomes a framework for current actions such as inadequate planning, minimal instructional activities, and little or no involvement in professional growth (73, 78). Various terms have been used to describe teachers who are victims of this process: static, stressed, incompetent, and burned out (2). Langer (44) warns that individuals who see themselves and their ecology as fate-filled tend to remain in a state of continuous deterioration.

Stressed teachers, especially those who have entered into a continuous pattern of burnout, seem to retreat from the process that they need most: the renewal cycle. Once teachers form negative life views and see little hope for improvement, they gradually pull back from meaningful personal and professional involvements (67, 78). Erikson (24) observes that bitterness and excessive guilt are symptomatic of adult impotence in the face of the generativity/despair crisis. Finding sources of renewal in one's personal achievements and in the progress seen in the ecology is critical to having a positive adult identity (43, 59). The erosion of teacher integrity that occurs during negative stress contributes to the formation of despair and, thus, greatly reduces the possibility of having useful renewal experiences (2, 24, 78).

The psychological isolation of parents from classroom events is directly related to stress. Parents are affected by whatever happens to their children, and the stress children experience at school is transferred to relationships at home. Parents react in many ways to excessive classroom stress; the result may be an increase in conflicts with their children, the development of negative attitudes toward the school, a reduction of involvement with the teacher, a reduction of effectiveness in other activities such as in the work place, and a loss of faith in the educational process (8, 32, 69). The three most alarming results of classroom stress as it impacts parents are these: (1) the alteration of their relationships with their children, (2) the increase in their isolation from what happens to their child in the classroom, and (3) the damage to the parental self-concept that can occur in such cases (29, 76).

The stress that children most often complain about to parents is that related to school failure or other dysfunctional events that occur in the classroom. When such complaints are continuous, intense, and clearly reflective of a lowered self-concept in the child, parents seem to change their orientation toward the child. Parents may become more rigid in their interactions with the child, reduce their support of the child, and place unreasonable demands on the child. Unless this type of parent-child relationship is corrected, additional stress emerges and the situation can become unmanageable (38, 55).

Alienation between parent and child is the most devastating of all possible consequences of stress on parents. The intensity of classroom stress can degrade the child and stimulate the conditions that promote alienation. This is especially pertinent to cases in which parents do not see the possibility of changing their child's situation in the classroom. For example, when parents have failed in their efforts to alleviate classroom stressors, such as peer conflicts or misconceptions by the teacher, they may withdraw their psychological involvement in the child's problem. This alienation tends to destroy both family integrity and any hope of improving the child's school position (5, 10).

Ultimately, parental self-concept is damaged by the negative stress the child experiences at school. Parents often blame themselves for what happens to the child. Another typical response is for parents to lay the blame totally on the teacher or the school administration. Parents with a low self-concept usually feel a sense of helplessness, an inability to analyze problems, and a corresponding sense of being overwhelmed. Irrational behaviors, such as withdrawing from school involvement, blaming the teacher, and formulating unreasonable requests of school officials, are the actions of insecure and stressed parents (29, 38).

Stress is an interactional process that is rarely confined to one context. It affects all those who are connected to the individuals involved and can even extend to systems that originally had little to do with the stress. Classroom stress is often the result of many sources that come together in the educational arena and, thus, it influences these same sources in various ways. Like a cancer, stress can spread through the school, family, and community in subtle, yet damaging ways. Research points out that reasoned behavior is the key antidote to stress, and because the classroom serves as a bridge between many systems, it is a logical place in which to apply the skills of management and control to alleviate the possible dangers of this destructive force.

Chapter 4
STRATEGIES FOR DEALING WITH CLASSROOM STRESS

The multiplicity of sources of classroom stress provides unlimited potential for dealing with the problem. A basic finding of stress research is that while many people seem prone to anxiety when certain events occur, many other people use stressors as challenges to improve their situation. Various studies suggest that people have more power to control stress than they commonly use (6, 25, 30, 64). Teachers face an uncommon situation in that they are confronted with a group situation in which the potential for stress is very high. Yet, teachers and other helping professionals have many resources to draw on in dealing with stress-related issues. Strategies for dealing with classroom stress can be organized into three categories: prevention strategies, resolution strategies, and extension strategies. The philosophical basis of these strategies includes the following points: (1) unhealthy stress that is pervasive and continuous is damaging to the teaching-learning process, (2) each person responds to stress in a unique way and her or his "style" of living must be accommodated, and (3) cooperative, supportive learning environments are desirable because they empower students and teachers to use stress in productive ways (5, 67, 77).

STRESS-PREVENTION STRATEGIES

The focus of stress-prevention strategies is on creating a context in which the emergence of negative stress is minimized. The extent to which negative stress can be prevented in the classroom depends on the actions of the participants and the substance of the learning environment (30). When teachers and students interact in productive, supportive classrooms, stress can be viewed and used in ways that promote learning development.

Preventing Teacher Stress

The key planner for positive learning arrangements is the teacher. If a teacher is constantly stressed, the potential for preventing stress in his/her classroom is limited. Thus, a teacher's personal-control orientation is critical in the design of any classroom program focusing on stress prevention. Langer (44) notes that a high control orientation results when the interaction between a person and her/his ecology produces a mindful approach to problem solving. Teachers can strengthen their control skills by refining their educational skills (including pedagogical, classroom management, and personal skills), strengthening their professional and personal support systems, and nurturing their self-concept through recognition of achievements and personal renewal activities (25, 29, 77).

Glasser (29) identifies several things that teachers can "control" in attempting to prevent stress: they should maintain good health, get adequate rest, practice good dietary habits, pursue interests that are personally rewarding, develop and maintain a time for self-reflection, construct and continually refine a positive mental health framework, and take an active supportive role in the community. The demands on teachers are so great that they must approach the maintenance of their control skills in a mindful manner. Figure 1 presents a self-assessment inventory for teachers to use in evaluating their stress-prevention status.

Figure 1
A Stress-Prevention Inventory for Teachers:
Focus on Control Skills

_____ I have consistent feelings of being overwhelmed.

_____ I have continuing problems with classroom management.

_____ I would characterize my personal life as very high in anxiety.

_____ I have very little control over my teaching situation.

_____ I seem to have many negative feelings about the students I teach.

_____ I never seem to have time to pursue interests that mean a great deal to me.

_____ I never really feel comfortable in the school in which I teach.

_____ I have not been involved in any professional renewal experiences recently.

_____ I do not spend much time interacting with peers on professional issues.

_____ I seem to have one health problem after another.

Affirmation of any of the above situations is reason for teachers to take action to strengthen their personal and professional control skills. When teachers find that they identify with four or more of the items on the inventory, they should seek out resources to use in building a renewal plan that will facilitate their revitalization. Classroom teachers need maximum control of themselves, their environment, and their interactions with students in order to promote a healthy classroom ecology (78).

Developing effective *interpersonal relationships* is certainly a major stress prevention strategy. Three elements of teachers' interpersonal dynamics are affect toward others, interaction patterns with others, and communication skills used in carrying out the teaching-learning process (14, 18, 31, 39). Negative interpersonal relationships damage the individual as well as the total group. Children have been observed to respond irrationally in settings in which teachers or parents are consistently punitive, restrictive, and degrading to the children. Studies of teacher personality patterns have noted that children's receptivity to instruction increases when teachers are positive and facilitative in their orientation (2, 46, 77).

Teacher affect is comprised of their perceptions and resulting actions toward others. Clearly, teachers who have positive views of their students are more likely to have productive relationships in the classroom, thus decreasing the chances of negative stress. When teachers expect students to do well, they seem to work harder at helping students achieve. The invitational learning environment begins with the teacher's attitudinal orientation toward students (43, 53, 67). The following affective areas of teaching should be reviewed by teachers on a regular basis:

1. What is my attitude toward the students I teach? Do I see them as capable/incapable, growing/deteriorating, inquisitive/stagnant?

2. What is my attitude toward teaching? Do I enjoy teaching? Do I look forward to trying out new ideas, or do I avoid new and challenging situations?

3. How do I view parents: as allies in the learning process or as people who should keep their distance from the classroom?

4. What is my perspective of the learning process? Do I see it as a "pouring in" process or as an inquiry-oriented process?

5. Do I have good attitudes toward my peers? Do I view them as a team or as obstacles to having an effective educational program?

Teachers can take a major step toward preventing stress by developing in themselves positive attitudes toward students, parents, and their peers. Purkey and Novak (67) note that when teachers view them as

39

capable and valuable members of the classroom, students perform effectively and the teacher engages in teaching at a highly intimate level.

A major deterrent to classroom stress is effective *classroom management*. Advance planning of how groups will function and how group members will be involved in the planning process maximizes the potential for stress prevention (14). Teachers have found the following management practices useful in creating productive learning environments: (1) making advance decisions about expected student behavior, (2) involving students and parents in the process of determining desired student behavior, (3) clarifying classroom rules as related to expected behaviors, (4) discussing the consequences of undesirable behavior, (5) continually refining the plan as is developmentally appropriate (18). Students and teachers tend to function best in cooperatively managed classrooms. Rigidly organized management systems often devote too much attention to negative behavior and too little to positive behavior.

The development of autonomy in students is the goal of all management practices. Thus, engaging students in monitoring their own behavior facilitates a productive teacher-student relationship. Cangelosi (14) recommends that teachers manage the instructional process and the learning environment in a way that prompts students to take on responsibilities appropriate to their developmental status. Research supports this position through findings that individuals who have control over their behavior are more successful in the learning process (25, 44). Strategies that promote positive student behavior include project-oriented instruction, displays of student-developed materials, opportunities for students to apply newly acquired skills in the community, and assignments that stimulate students to "plan" their involvement in the learning process (14, 18, 39, 67).

Elements of the group management process that can become stress points in the classroom are explicated by Swick (77): negative student behavior patterns, large class sizes, poor time usage, poorly planned instruction, rigid teaching practices, and inadequate learning resources. It is clear that teachers can prevent a great deal of stress by anticipating stressors and planning so as to minimize their influence in the classroom. Using their knowledge of student development, pedagogical practices, and classroom design, teachers can manage many issues by organizing a proactive approach to anticipated stressors (77). Figure 2 presents a list of classroom management practices that have been useful in preventing needless classroom stress.

Well-managed classrooms give students the security of knowing what is expected of them, the strategies for reaching these expectations in a reasonable manner, and a context in which they can develop self-management skills. Positive, orderly, and inviting classrooms reduce stress

Figure 2
Management Practices for Preventing Classroom Stress

---

1. Involve students and parents in the development of classroom procedures and rules.

2. Develop management guidelines that are appropriate to the age and cultural context of the students.

3. Emphasize the development of self-discipline in the classroom management plan.

4. Communicate desired behaviors, expectations, and rules to students on a regular basis.

5. Be flexible in implementing the management plan; remember that situations change, students develop new interests, and each person is unique.

6. Utilize cooperative learning strategies that promote the involvement of all students.

7. Review the management plan periodically to assure that needed refinements are made.

8. Know the behavior of the students as much as possible and integrate this knowledge into classroom management planning.

9. Anticipate potential problems and design scenarios for responding to them.

10. Evaluate the plan at least once a year, using the results to refine and improve it.

---

and increase formal and informal learning time (18, 59, 77).

A static, unmotivated teacher is more likely to be victimized by stress than is a growing, developing teacher (77, 78). Case studies of burned-out teachers reveal that they were victims of stress primarily because they had failed to continue their growth and development. The continual renewal of teachers' professional and personal development skills is an effective strategy for preventing classroom stress (2, 78).

Professional and personal renewal activities can be directed toward preventing or resolving stress-related issues. Swick and Hanley (78) suggest the following techniques: developing a good understanding of who you are as a person and as a professional, developing and utilizing basic stress-management strategies, organizing the environment to prevent unhealthy stress, using your professional peers as resource people in dealing with different stressors, defining personal and professional priorities and establishing a plan for carrying them out, maintaining sound physical and mental health, and planning for self-renewal activities.

An extension of stress prevention is the *proactive use of stress-inducing elements as a challenge*. Evidence suggests that teachers who turn problems into creative solutions, enjoy experimenting with new ideas, try new hobbies and pursue new interests, and respond totally to the situation they face not only reduce their stress but also increase their energy level for productive tasks. The realization that one is able to move beyond a prevention/resolution orientation gives teachers many new insights into all aspects of their lives (2).

Students tend to follow the adult lead in terms of solving problems and responding to stress. Teachers who feel secure about their identity, respond to conflict in creative and viable ways, and remain growing, developing individuals have a profoundly positive influence on student functioning.

Preventing Environmental Stress

Each classroom takes on an identity that influences the participants in many ways. The combination of the various interactions in the classroom is often called the *learning climate*. Studies of this classroom climate reveal factors that create stress in children: a disorganized physical setting, negative human interactions, ineffective teacher-leadership, a rigid time schedule, a punitive psychological atmosphere, deficient social arrangements, a poor curriculum, and limited instructional strategies (31, 37, 51, 57, 76). References to the climate of the classroom are most appropriate because it is the overall feeling that people have about an environment that determines their interaction patterns in that environment (33, 34, 44). When the psychological climate is such that students feel isolated, controlled, or unimportant, their anxiety level is certain to be high and their learning system negatively influenced (5, 10).

Creating a psychologically healthy climate in the classroom is a significant step toward the prevention of classroom stress. While many of the elements of a positive classroom climate may seem to be intangible, certain qualitative factors have been identified as positively influencing student behavior: teacher personality; an ordered, but sensitive and flexible learning environment; a high value on the personal traits and talents of students and teachers; an active and expressive learning ecology; warm, sensitive interactions among the participants in the classroom; and a feeling of shared ownership of the classroom (51, 53, 59, 61). Research is clear on the teacher's role in establishing a positive and productive climate for learning and development. Studies on teacher personality orientation indicate that democratic, warm, open, organized, and sensitive behaviors are effective in promoting a healthy classroom setting (59, 61, 67).

Swick (77) delineates student behaviors that should be promoted in order to foster positive mental health in the classroom:

1. Promote a sense of *success* in students, especially those students who have a history of failure.

2. Encourage students to be *pleasant, friendly, and positive* in their interactions with each other.

3. Promote situations in which students take notice of the *positive things* they all achieve.

4. Encourage students to *develop a special talent* or favorite hobby and share it with their peers.

5. Encourage students to *express their feelings* in a constructive manner.

6. Promote a "learning by making mistakes" attitude in students. Support their efforts to *learn through failure* and encourage them to support this effort in their peers.

7. Promote a *caring attitude* in students by involving them in activities in which they reach out to care for others.

8. Encourage students to *engage in cooperative learning* by planning project teams and peer learning situations.

9. Promote student *self-discipline* by having them plan their weekly work schedule.

10. Encourage students to *develop all of their learning skills* by involving them in various types of instructional activities.

In promoting a positive classroom climate, teachers should focus on the following: creating a supportive atmosphere in which helping relationships can flourish, helping each student develop her or his unique place in the classroom, modeling the kinds of positive behavior that students should develop, staying in touch with student feelings and integrating their ideas into the classroom management plan, allowing for the individuation of student learning styles, and maintaining positive interactions with students (75). In positive classroom environments students are more likely to succeed, develop effective coping skills, and learn to use stress in challenging, creative ways (77, 78).

Time is an important element of the classroom ecology. Effective time management of classroom activities can preclude the emergence of many

43

stressors, such as student confusion over what they should be doing or student anxiety over not being able to complete a task within a time frame that is too rigid (5, 7, 77). In managing time, several complex elements need to be considered: the developmental status of students, their cultural orientation, the nature of the content being taught, time usage practices as supported by research, special student needs, available resources, and the time frame provided by the school system (18). In addition, teacher perceptions of time usage significantly influence student behavior. For example, a teacher who feels that time is to be rigidly defined not only precludes student involvement in learning time management but also may be causing unhealthy stress in the classroom (5, 21, 55).

While it is unlikely that teachers can design perfect time systems, it is feasible to pursue the development of a workable time scheme. Hall (33) provides several insights on how human functioning can be improved through productive time management. He emphasizes the importance of knowing the time pattern of the people you are dealing with and then integrating that knowledge into your involvements with the group. For example, within any given class there are many different time systems in operation: body time, clock time, cultural time, and school time. Insightful teachers usually gather data on these time systems as the students function during the early part of the school year and then adapt their time plans accordingly. Usually a group time frame will emerge from the class's behavior, and instructional planning can be modified to make use of this process. Further, when teachers recognize these varying time orientations, they provide students with a positive role model on effective time management (18, 29, 75). Some examples of poor time usage are as follows:

1. Giving students a complex task to do first thing in the morning (33).
2. Scheduling time so tightly that students always feel hurried (19).
3. Failing to clarify for students how time is to be used, thus causing much anxiety (55).
4. Making all of the decisions on time usage and failing to involve students in this important aspect of learning (14).
5. Expecting students to abide by time frames that are developmentally inappropriate for their life stage (19, 20).

A great deal of classroom stress can be prevented by developing a viable approach to time management. The following guidelines should be useful in preparing a proactive time plan:

44

1. Assess your personal time usage orientation. Are you an effective planner of time? Do you always feel stressed because of time pressures? Teachers who feel stressed by their own time usage need to master this aspect of time management before attempting to resolve problems related to the school or classroom (2, 29, 78).

2. Take stock of the parameters of school time. The broad time frame of the school day can be used as a basis for planning your particular time-management system (77).

3. Gather data on the various time systems that students exhibit in their behavior patterns. Are there some common time usage patterns you have observed that can be integrated into your classroom management plan? Are there special student needs that must be considered (33)?

4. Examine your expectations of how students should use time. Are these expectations appropriate, realistic? How might they be refined and improved (67)?

5. Observe actual student behaviors related to time usage. Are students in need of experiences that will improve their time-management skills (75)?

6. Involve students in making decisions about how to use classroom time in a productive manner. Students who are continually involved in learning how to plan time schedules usually are more task oriented and higher achievers (77).

7. Plan for meaningful social learning to occur during each day. Time devoted to accepting student ideas, nurturing special needs, and responding to students' personal needs is time well spent (59).

8. Maintain a flexible approach to time usage; rigidity only increases stress and reduces student motivation to learn (7).

Stress can also be minimized by using space in a viable way. Research indicates that crowding, poorly planned classroom space, and inflexible use of space produce negative stress (18, 33). Just as important as physical space is the psychosocial space that students and teachers need in order to relate classroom learning to their individual situations. What is important is that each student should develop a sense of importance and acceptance in the classroom. Psychological rejection or isolation is more damaging than is limited physical space because if one is not connected mentally to classroom events, productive learning is precluded (10).

People define space differently by using their cultural, familial, and individual reference points as bases for action. For example, some students are "space sharers" by experience and have difficulty in relating to the notion of "private space." Other students are restrictive of their space and find it threatening when people intrude (33). Accommodating the various styles of space usage is difficult, but critical to creating a positive learning environment.

Organizing the classroom so that students participate in designing the space arrangement is a valuable strategy for integrating different ways of living into the curriculum. Additional strategies for making classroom space a viable part of the program are these: designing learning areas that have clearly stated functions, creating transition areas in which students can move with ease from one activity to another, planning areas of the classroom that students can "complete" with their design ideas, displaying student products in the room and throughout the school, integrating your "self" into the classroom space by displaying things you have developed, and developing a renewal approach so space usage adjustments can be made as needed throughout the school year (9, 14, 39, 67).

A hallmark of healthy development in children and adolescents is that the individual senses he or she is "special," "important," and "valued" by the significant people in the ecology (9). Another benchmark occurs when the individual senses that a common ground exists in the interactions that take place in the ecology (22, 23). The psychosocial space of the classroom should be designed so that students can construct an image of themselves as unique to the classroom and yet "connected" in a sensitive, caring manner to the people and events that occur (9, 67). The following strategies have proved effective in achieving this personal and social competence in students: conducting regular "share sessions" during which each student contributes something she or he has developed, interacting with students according to a planned schedule, recognizing individual student achievements in various skill and talent areas, encouraging individuation of student interests, and utilizing many cooperative learning activities and projects (10, 14, 73). Figure 3 presents an inventory of items that can be used to assess the classroom in terms of poor space usage or space planning.

Learning how to care for self, others, and the environment is a key stress-prevention practice. In terms of human relationships, the classroom should become a source of support and nurturance. Three behavior patterns that should be the focus of a proactive classroom are nurturing, helping, and caring (10, 61, 67). *Nurture* means to facilitate a person or process through supportive actions. People who function in supportive contexts exhibit few stress syndromes and are generally peak performers. Recent research shows that cooperative, team-oriented approaches to teaching and learning are very successful in strengthening student learn-

46

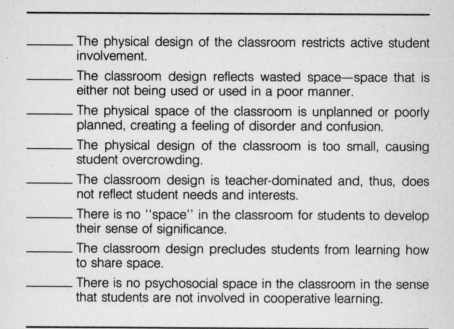

Figure 3
Inventory of Space Usage Practices
That Can Create Classroom Stress

_____ The physical design of the classroom restricts active student involvement.

_____ The classroom design reflects wasted space—space that is either not being used or used in a poor manner.

_____ The physical space of the classroom is unplanned or poorly planned, creating a feeling of disorder and confusion.

_____ The physical design of the classroom is too small, causing student overcrowding.

_____ The classroom design is teacher-dominated and, thus, does not reflect student needs and interests.

_____ There is no "space" in the classroom for students to develop their sense of significance.

_____ The classroom design precludes students from learning how to share space.

_____ There is no psychosocial space in the classroom in the sense that students are not involved in cooperative learning.

ing (61, 67). Human beings appear to function best when they feel a sense of security and warmth in their interactions with others. In fact, it is only recently that research on the psychosocial makeup of people has revealed the importance of fostering warm, pleasant human interaction patterns. It is clear that when individuals are in nurturing settings, they have little need to "waste" energy on defensive living and, thus, can actually generate new levels of productivity through their positive involvement with others (23, 34, 38).

Strategies that promote nurturing human relationships in the classroom include the following: becoming sensitive to the socioemotional facets of learning, integrating socioemotional learning experiences into the curriculum, and developing a clear understanding of the importance of sensitive, warm interactions among students and teachers (77). Children and adolescents should be encouraged to study their behavior in terms of how they nurture themselves and others. The use of content that sheds light on how nurturing increases a person's human potential and actual human functioning might increase student sensitivity to this

47

area of learning development (33, 34).

Involving students in helping roles is a very effective way of preventing useless stress. Projects in which students tutor, work with younger children, put on a play, produce a classroom newspaper, or take part in a myriad of other such activities encourage them to extend their reach into reality-based situations and to become more sensitive to the many talents of their peers (61, 67). The stress that can emerge from such involvement is a healthy form of stress in that it revolves around the individual's struggle to carry out the process of individuation within a context that requires new insights and new growth (22, 23). When behaviors such as empathetic listening, teaming, sensitive responding, and cooperative learning are prompted, students are at least pointed in a direction that holds the potential to strengthen their linkages with significant others (10).

The truly caring person directs her or his energy toward creative ends. Individuals who must feel they are needed in order for their ecology to work effectively usually have a healthy form of stress. It is alienation that produces great stress in students and teachers. Sociometric studies of student functioning in classrooms reveal that children who are isolated from the ecology experience extreme stress and have the most trouble in school (4, 12, 13, 41). In proposing a "curriculum for caring," Bronfenbrenner (10) notes that it is possible for a child to progress through the entire school system without having to make a significant contribution to others. Research supports Bronfenbrenner's hypothesis in that the major cause of adolescent mental health problems is the sense of alienation from a meaningful existence (20, 23). Figure 4 presents examples of classroom strategies that teachers have found useful in promoting a curriculum for caring.

A stimulating, varied, and involvement-oriented curriculum directs student energy into creative actions. Programs that are overly mechanistic and devoid of meaning produce much boredom, which is a great stress producer. A classroom setting that is "inviting," designed to involve students in acquiring control of their learning, and oriented toward a positive use of stress is certain to produce many capable learners (77).

Preventing Student Stress

Even in the most ideal classroom, some children develop negative stress. A variety of factors—for example, neglect at home, poor health, or personal deficits—can be at work in such cases (5). Research provides some clues as to sources of individual stress and points to some plausible strategies for preventing it. The following sources of stress arise even in quality situations: lack of control skills, low self-concept, poor interper-

Figure 4
Strategies for Promoting a Curriculum for Caring

1. Modeling caring behaviors by taking an interest in student concerns and problems.

2. Expecting students to behave in caring ways by including content on it in the daily instructional program.

3. Educating parents about the importance of students' developing "caring" attitudes and behaviors, and providing them with strategies they can use in this endeavor.

4. Making the "care" of the classroom a significant part of student learning and development.

5. Making "care" of self and others a priority of the instructional program.

6. Having students study the community in regard to caring behaviors they observe or needs they identify.

7. Involving students in caring roles in the community, such as helping at nursing homes and participating in community cleanup projects and other improvement activities.

8. Expanding student awareness of the need for global caring; having them identify positive world projects and determine needs they might influence in a positive way.

sonal skills, an extremely passive life style, and deficient cognitive and language skills (12, 21, 41, 51).

Of all the characteristics prevalent in stress-prone children and adolescents, the most pervasive one is self-concept. Students who are easily stressed have a low self-concept. They see themselves as powerless and others as sources of fear (67). The fostering of positive self-concepts in students is an effective preventer of unhealthy stress.

One way to foster positive developments in others is to model such actions in the classroom. For example, Honig states:

Demonstrate self-control and coping skills yourself. Be fair and sensitive to differences and problems . . . . If a teacher's voice is exasperated, whiny, disappointed, aggrieved, or angry fairly often, the children learn that these are acceptable modes of coping with stress. (38, p. 55)

Children and adolescents find that teachers who are good at using the environment in a proactive way are sources of strength in defining their own self-image (29. For example, teachers who use control skills, empathetic listening, and positive socioeducational strategies to deal with stress are more likely to influence students in this direction, in contrast to teachers whose reactions to stress are always anxiety ridden (7).

Another way of promoting positive self-concept development in students is to interact with them in ways that support the emergence of this process. Students often define themselves in the way they are treated. Provide each student with the attention that stimulates a sense of warmth and security in him/her. For example, Mrs. Arnold keeps notes on the interests each child in her fifth grade is pursuing. She finds ways to reinforce those interests and to get the students involved in recognizing their peers' special talents. Studies of children and adults who have interests beyond school and work indicate that their self-esteem is high and their stress low (48, 54, 84).

Teaching children about self-care and self-image-making is a critical part of their basic education. Understanding who we are, what we can become, and how we can acquire self-development skills is a part of what might be called a student's self-concept education (25, 29, 67). Four self-concept areas directly related to stress prevention are self, social, cognitive, and affective development. Self-development behaviors worth pursuing in instructional contexts include acquiring a persistence orientation, developing an optimistic future view, internalizing a high tolerance toward frustration, and mastering self-confidence-building skills. Social behaviors that can be encouraged in the classroom include sharing ideas related to group functioning, discussing stress-related concerns with the teacher, helping others deal with stress, and communicating skillfully. Cognitive behaviors that are connected to the development of student self-concept are functioning autonomously, focusing on issues at hand, have a reflectively oriented thinking style, and forming a strong, inner control orientation. Finally, the following areas of affective learning need equal attention: understanding the socioemotional process, expressing feelings in a constructive manner, dealing proactively with the feelings of others, and developing a healthy sense of humor (7). These skill areas can be integrated into instructional activities and fostered through various teacher-student interactions.

Helping children and adolescents develop control skills is another means of preventing negative stress. Passive, fatalistic, and reactive students develop high levels of stress and appear to have few skills to alleviate their problems (15, 17, 25, 37). Students who very effectively cope with stress or prevent it have highly developed skills. In assisting students to develop their control skills, teachers can focus on three strategies: (1) providing situations in which students must make decisions—

that is, they must take control of some aspect of their lives; (2) providing instruction on the decision-making process and engaging students in applying the process to life situations that are important to them; and (3) guiding students toward using feedback from experience as a means of refining and improving their control skills (77). Following are examples of how to apply these three skill-building strategies to the instructional process:

1. Incorporate a student planning component into your course format. Have students plan their schedules for completing assignments. This process can be extended to involving students in planning various aspects of their personal lives, too.

2. Involve students in thinking about their behavior: have them focus on their strong points as well as areas that need improvement. Extend this activity by having students develop a plan to improve their classroom behavior.

3. Develop problem-solving situations appropriate for your students, and have them make decisions regarding the resolution of the problems. Have them justify their decisions and deal with the results.

4. Have students conduct a stress-prevention study of the classroom. Have them identify key stressors and propose ways to prevent stress from detracting from the learning process.

5. When students fail at a task or are having a series of difficulties in the classroom, have them identify positive ways in which they can use their experience to overcome the stress.

Langer (44) offers some key insights on helping people build control skills. She states that control building is essentially about the "control of oneself and one's perceptions of reality" (44, p. 13). In other words, it is critical that children receive guidance in building a perceptual orientation that makes them feel confident about dealing with life. For example, a child who sees school as threatening is more likely to experience stress than is a child who views school as an exciting adventure. To simply bypass the child's incorrect perception is of little value because this perception is what s/he bases her or his behavior on. Before this child can acquire a more productive control orientation toward school, s/he must change her or his perceptual basis. Langer (44) notes that control emerges in people as they are able to see a relationship between their behavior and certain desired outcomes. Thus, students who have many successful experiences in controlling stress, preventing stress, and turning stress into creative outlets are developing a strong orientation that will serve them throughout life (34). Figure 5 presents a list of behaviors that teachers can assess with regard to students' control orientation.

Figure 5
Inventory of Student Behaviors
Related to Their Control Orientation

---

1. The student has an extremely short attention span for his/her stage of development.

2. The student is constantly irritated by even the smallest of classroom events.

3. The student gives up easily in the face of new challenges; he or she lacks the breadth of skills for dealing with change.

4. The student is excessivley withdrawn and resists efforts to involve him or her in group activities.

5. The student is negative in most of his/her social interactions; he or she does not make friends in a natural way.

6. The student fails to complete routine tasks on a continuing basis.

7. The student is extremely nervous and seems unable to achieve even minimum equilibrium in terms of classroom functioning.

8. The student constantly blames others and distorts feedback in such a way as to reinforce a failure-oriented, "I can't do it" behavior syndrome.

9. The student is very isolated from the mainstream of classroom events; he or she has few friends and is lacking in skills for using the environment effectively.

10. The student is prone to using attention-getting behavior in stressful situations.

Students who exhibit more than a few of the behaviors listed in Figure 5 are certain to spend their lives in cycles of anxiety-ridden functioning. By involving students in developing healthy behavior patterns, these stress-oriented cycles can be prevented. But in order to develop viable perceptual patterns, students need a great deal of input on how to function proactively. This needs to begin during early childhood with many diverse experiences with warm, supportive adults. Large doses of early success in dealing with self and the environment provide children with the experiential foundation to approach life positively. In addition, children need to observe and experience positive ways of facing difficult situations. As children construct schemes for controlling their behavior on a proactive basis, they will see how to deal with many aspects of life (9, 44).

The control-building process initiated during the early childhood years can be extended throughout students' school life. In the elementary school, students can be encouraged to think analytically, communicate clearly, and participate constructively, both inside and outside the classroom. Older students need continued encouragement in developing an anticipatory life style that is founded on a positive, exploratory, and mindful learning orientation (8, 29, 44, 77).

A significant part of acquiring a sense of harmony with life is learning to conceptualize and articulate how one feels about particular events (38). Students who develop their skills in *clarifying and expressing emotional feelings* can avoid much stress. In many cases this process can be a part of the natural flow of classroom events. For example, a student who feels secure in sharing with the teacher that s/he needs time to complete an assignment because of problems at home is certainly more likely to prevent stress than is a student who is fearful of sharing such thoughts. There are cases in which professional help is needed for students who have serious emotional problems. Most classrooms, however, are ideal places in which to foster positive emotional expressiveness in students (7). Honig (38) and Abood (1) recommend several strategies for promoting positive emotional development in students:

1. Involving students in various healthy emotional experiences appropriate to their developmental status: sharing feelings about achievements, celebrating special events, contributing to the well-being of others, and participating in community activities.

2. Acknowledging students' feelings as real, valid, and important to the functioning of a worthwhile classroom. Let students know they are not alone in having negative feelings. Help them learn how to express these feelings and how to create positive outcomes from such feelings.

3. Involving students in dramatic activities through which they can deal with human emotions in many ways and explore various positive options to solving problems. The integration of affective learning into classroom instructional activities helps students see that this facet of life is a significant part of learning.

4. Encouraging students to use active listening in their interactions with others. Show them how this works. That is, have them listen

to the ideas and behaviors of other students and use this information to formulate positive ways of relating to others. For example, a student may be hurting another student by name-calling; have that student think about how he or she would react to such treatment.

5. Using bibliotherapy to introduce students to ways that other people have successfully dealt with various human emotions. Be cautious in selecting literature that provides students with ideas that are pertinent to their life stage.

Three additional strategies for preventing classroom stress are these: using positive interpersonal dynamics, using group and individual meetings to foster a productive team feeling, and instructing students on ways to develop a balanced life style (9, 14, 20, 75).

The prevention of negative interpersonal dynamics is linked to having a healthy stress situation in the classroom. Designing situations in which students must see the positive side of their peers is one way to accomplish this goal. Additional techniques include putting students into working groups in which their teaming is essential to successful task completion; having role exchanges in which students experience leadership and followership; and encouraging students to help each other to improve their relationship patterns (14, 75). Students should be involved in "studying" their interpersonal ecology and in taking steps to refine it as needed. For example, Mrs. Randolph met with three students to encourage them to include John and Betty in their recess activities. She continued this guidance process using small group instruction to develop the social skills of all five students. In discussions, she emphasized the importance of developing an understanding of and a sensitivity to the talents and needs of others. This continued nurturance of the interpersonal facet of the classroom helps to prevent stress.

By meeting with individual students and with the entire group in class meetings, teachers can foster a positive classroom climate. Individual meetings can be used to clear the air, resolve minor issues, and bolster a particular student's self-image. Many times a student simply needs to know that s/he has been doing a good job. Classroom meetings can be used to take care of common concerns and to build a sense of unity and harmony. For example, a great deal of emotional baggage can build up in any classroom. Having a regular time to sort out issues and to refine rules and relationships is important to the group's mental health (67).

Students receive many different messages about what is important in life. For example, it is common for some teachers to tell students not to worry about grades but rather to focus on learning. Yet, at the end of school, all of the important awards given are based on grades. Thus, in theory and in practice teachers should promote a balanced life style for students. Encourage students to take care of their health, nurture their affective self, maintain consistent physical activity, pursue recreational interests, and work at being academically capable. Students who are healthy, are involved in at least some of the classroom functions, and have a positive self-image are not likely to be easily stressed.

STRESS-RESOLUTION STRATEGIES

It is common for many students and teachers to face excessive negative stress. For them it is not a question of prevention but one of finding a resolution to their predicament. How can teachers resolve stressful situation? What can be done to alter a classroom context that fosters high levels of negative stress? What hope is there for the student who is already experiencing a great deal of stress? Questions such as these are dealt with in this section on resolving stressful situations.

Resolving Teacher Stress

Like any behavior pattern, a stressful life style becomes internalized and accepted as a way of life. In some instances the only stimulus for change is the eventual burnout that accompanies the stress cycle (2). Recognition that one is under a great deal of stress is the first event that must happen if the stress-resolution process is to take place in a productive way. Unfortunately, a hurried and stressful mode of functioning is often seen as the only way to survive the many challenges of teaching. It is true that teachers and other helping professionals face more stressors than do people involved in less demanding tasks. However, it is also realistic and essential to understand that stressed teachers are generally ineffective in their job roles and often harm students by injecting this stress into the classroom (2, 18, 46). Figure 6 reviews some of the major symptoms of teachers who are under excessive stress. An elaboration of these stress symptoms can be found in *Stress and the Classroom Teacher* (78) and *Teacher Renewal: Revitalization of Classroom Teachers* (see Additional Readings).

Stressed teachers, those who exhibit the behaviors listed in Figure 6 or other such behavior patterns, must ask themselves these questions: Why am I behaving this way? What is the cause of my irritation? Getting to the source of this behavior is critical to identifying the stressors that are having such a negative impact on their lives. The reasons for stress vary and depend on the personality and context of each teacher. For example, some teachers might be bothered by a paperwork overload, while others absorb it in a creative manner. Mrs. Williams found that her overload

Figure 6
Teacher Behaviors Indicative of Excessive Stress

---

1. Being constantly irritated with even the smallest disruptions in the classroom.
2. Focusing only on students' negative behaviors and constantly making punitive remarks to students.
3. Talking at students in sharp, short phrases and displaying little sensitivity for student feelings.
4. Being very defensive in responding to student questions and making students feel belittled in their attempts to learn.
5. Constantly hurrying students to complete tasks and being very impatient with students who diverge from the norm.

---

resulted from trying to meet family needs, take care of her sick mother, and remain capable in her teaching. She knew she was being "short" with the students and was always complaining to others about her hectic life. A visit to her family physician confirmed what she knew: something had to give! Mrs. Williams had achieved the first step in the stress-resolution process: *identifying the source of her stress.*

Once identified, *the stressor must be examined thoroughly* to determine how it is creating a negative situation. In Mrs. Williams's case, the issue was clear: there was not enough of her to meet all of the demands that existed in her life space. The answer may be more complex in other situations in which negative attitudes are involved or an individual has allowed the problem to become a ritual in his or her life.

After the nature of the stress has been clarified, it is time to initiate a planning scheme. Initially, the individual needs to *explore various ways to alleviate the problem.* By exploring various alternatives, one can acquire a true picture of steps to take that will work effectively. Mrs. Williams, for example, sought advice from her pastor, her brothers, and the counselor at the school district office. Of course, there were many suggestions on how she could resolve the problem. Once she had adequate input, Mrs. Williams began the next step, which was to *identify solutions in a priority sequence* based on what she valued and what was feasible, given her situation. As a result of her effort, she formulated three objectives that would greatly reduce her stress: (1) to acquire help in caring for her mother, (2) to reduce her school duties for this year, and (3) to develop a hobby that she could pursue at her leisure.

56

When a stress-resolution plan has been developed, it is vital to *explore all available resources for use in implementing it*. Mrs. Williams, for example, sought help from her brothers in sharing the load of caring for their mother. She met with her two daughters and gained agreement on dividing house chores among the three of them. Her principal agreed to release her from committee work for the year. She made real progress with her plan, but she realized that continual monitoring of her approach to life would be essential if she were to make long-term gains. She was, of course, correct in her recognition of *the need for continued self-assessment*. Habits are hard to change, and while a plan helps to initiate the change process, it takes many intentional efforts to reorganize one's life focus. Breaking patterns takes work because verbal and nonverbal behavioral patterns are deeply internalized. In fact, there are many behaviors that we might be able to refine but can never completely change. The important point is that the individual has to find her or his mode of functioning harmoniously in various settings.

Not all cases are resolved as easily as Mrs. Williams's. She obviously had a good history of using feedback for productive purposes. Some teachers might find that they need more in-depth assistance in dealing with stress. It is clear though that the stress-resolution process can be used to solve many problems and, thus, add to the renewal of teacher self-image. Mrs. Williams sums it up nicely: "It took a lot of energy, humility, and humor, but my students have noticed a new Mrs. Williams, one they like to be around and talk with."

Resolving Environmental Stress

Classroom-specific stressors often emerge as a result of the interaction of many forces: available space and resources, scheduling limitations, the handling of transitions, emotional climate, and the actual interpersonal dynamics of the participants (5). Once classroom stress occurs at an intense level, it influences so many elements that it may be difficult to sort out and manage them (47). For example, a space shortage might have caused a great deal of hostility in the classroom. However, once the hostility has emerged, it, in turn, might prompt the teacher to mistakenly tighten the daily schedule in an attempt to restore order. Yet, the rigid schedule prompts even more hostility that can create a cycle of increasing rigidity, stress, and disruptive behavior. This example serves to focus on the importance of teachers' being continually involved in studying their classroom ecology. Figure 7 presents some of the symptoms of classrooms that are under severe stress.

Figure 7
Symptoms of Excessive Classroom Stress

---

1. High levels of overt student anxiety are expressed through aggression, hostility, and other antisocial, degrading behaviors.
2. There is excessive chaos; order and harmony seem nonexistent.
3. Major problems exist with task completion—that is, very few students seem able to complete key assignments.
4. Negative interpersonal relationships are pervasive—that is, student interactions are negative in nature on a continuing basis.
5. Unusual passivity is evidenced in such student behavior patterns as asking few questions, engaging in little dialogue, and exhibiting an overall fear of exploring even the simplest of new ideas.

When teachers *recognize that classroom stress has reached an unhealthy level*, they can start to resolve the problem by noting the indicators that directed them to this realization. *Teacher observation of factors in the ecology that may be causing stress* is essential to laying the foundation for a resolution. One signal that a stressor is classroom specific is that a number of students are behaving in stressed ways (67). Mr. Yang, for example, observed that many students were overly anxious on Thursdays. He finally held a class meeting to discuss the situation and found that the students were very bothered by having all their tests on Fridays. Listening to students' concerns, having peers visit and study the classroom, and videotaping class sessions are additional techniques for gaining insight on sources of classroom stress (18).

Once possible sources of classroom stress have been identified, teachers can *explore various ways to resolve the situation*. Given feedback from his students, Mr. Yang reorganized his testing schedule to include Wednesdays. He also designed other ways of assessing student performance so as to reduce negative student feelings regarding tests. Other teachers resolve classroom stress in the following ways: altering negative teacher behaviors, redesigning space plans, changing instructional techniques, decreasing the psychological rigidity of the classroom climate, increasing student involvement in the decision-making process, refining the time schedule of daily or weekly activities, and implementing changes in the curriculum (7, 77, 78).

The resolution of classroom-related stressors is a continuing process; it requires *dealing with the observed source of the problem as well as*

58

taking proactive steps to prevent future problems. It should also be noted that many stressed classrooms are the result of combinations of problems that require close analysis and long-range planning. Figure 8 summarizes the major steps that teachers should take to resolve classroom-specific stress.

Figure 8
Steps for Resolving Classroom-Specific Stress

1. Recognize classroom-specific stress symptoms.
2. Identify the stressors that appear to be classroom-specific.
3. Analyze the possible sources of the classroom stress.
4. Formulate a plan to resolve classroom stress.
5. Implement the plan.
6. Continually monitor the classroom climate.

Resolving Student Stress

Beyond classroom-specific stress is that stress that is unique to certain students, as evidenced by their responses to various situations in or out of the classroom. Individual students can be under stress for many reasons: frustration in dealing with developmental changes, feelings of rejection, serious conflicts in the home, health problems, inability to achieve academic expectations, overload resulting from excessive work and school demands, and other socioemotional situations (11, 16, 19, 20). Some stressors are experienced by many students and can be dealt with in group contexts. Other stress situations are experienced uniquely by individual students and should be handled sensitively and in a confidential manner (7). Figure 9 presents the steps teachers should take to help students resolve stressful situations.

Teachers must *understand the major sources of stress* for the students they teach. While there are common stressors that all students experience, there are also stress sources unique to certain life stages and possibly to particular schools and communities (82). For example, peer relationships become more significant as students enter adolescence. Students living in poverty may experience a basic-needs-deficiency type of stress, while upper income students are more likely to experience stress related to intense academic pressure. Students might also experience

Figure 9
Steps for Resolving Student Stress

---

1. Recognize the major sources of stress experienced by students in the age and developmental span you teach.
2. Know the basic behavior patterns of the students you teach.
3. Continually observe student participation in the classroom.
4. Identify the suspected student stress problem.
5. Validate the problem through study and analysis of the situation.
6. Formulate a plan to assist the student in resolving the stress.
7. Implement the plan carefully and sensitively.
8. Continually monitor the situation to ensure that the student is making positive progress.

---

cultural conflict when their identity is built on values different from what is expected in the school or classroom. A number of sources for improving one's professional knowledge of student stress are listed in the Bibliography.

An extension of knowing significant sources of student stress is *knowing the basic behavior patterns of the students one teaches* (77). Teachers need to ask themselves questions such as the following: What are my students like? What are their interests and talents? What are some of the typical stressors they face? How do they deal with stress? In coming to know individual students, similar questions can be used to acquire a picture of what might be called their typical behavior. Only when teachers have an understanding of how students usually function can they establish a reference point for noticing atypical behavior. One of the great failures of schools is that the number of students who go unnoticed in the classroom is increasing. In order to know their students, teachers must have regular interactions with them.

Teachers who are sensitive to the classroom's affective climate *observe student participation in classroom events on a continuing basis* (8, 77). For example, Mrs. Nadine takes time every day to watch how individual students function. "I can spot many problems before they become major situations," she says. Observing students with regard to their attitudes, physical functioning, social interactions, and academic involvement provides teachers with a "mental map" of expected actions. Major changes

60

in mood, performance, and interactions are usually symbolic of some form of student stress (7).

When teachers have a picture of how students usually function, they can *identify clear alterations in student behaviors*. For example, John is usually very eager to take the lead on almost any classroom project. Yet, during the past two weeks he has rarely volunteered for any leadership role. Another example is Kim who typically completes all of her work on time. Recently, however, she has been turning her work in late and has failed to complete several key tasks. When a student's behavior changes from normal ranges to the extreme, teachers can take note of this discrepancy and identify a situation that needs possible attention (21). Diligent observation of student behavior patterns can lead teachers to early intervention and, thus, the resolution of minor stress that if left unattended might become a crisis.

Once a teacher suspects that a student is confronting a stressor, *validation can be carried out by analyzing the situation*. Through such careful analysis of student problems, teachers can identify and confirm stress-related situations that may be influencing student behavior in a negative manner (77). The following example helps highlight this facet of the stress-resolution process:

Miss Claring had suspected that Rene was not getting enough sleep or was watching too much television, or possibly both processes were at work. Rene's mother had not come to the recent conference so she had not been able to tell her about this concern. She called Rene's mother and shared with her that Rene just wasn't doing her work as usual and seemed to be very tired during school. She found out that Rene's mother was also concerned but had been tending to her sick husband. "I'll make sure she gets her sleep and give her more attention," she told Miss Claring.

Sometimes a suspicion will prove to be erroneous, but early assessment of any potentially negative situation is warranted. It is also important to recognize that some stressed students face complex predicaments, and the resolution to their problems may take some time and involve some strategic planning. For example, Anita had been severely neglected for several years, and only recently was she placed in a good foster home. Her teacher, by taking an active interest in Anita's life, was able to help place her with good foster parents. Yet, it will take some thoughtful planning and a great deal of attention to nurture Anita toward a more positive life experience.

When *developing plans to resolve student stress*, a key guideline is to focus on helping students resolve as many of their problems themselves as is feasible for their developmental status and particular life context (25, 29). While it may appear to be easier to take control and resolve the issue for the student, it is critical that the student become proficient in resolving his or her problems and, thus, learn the skills necessary for future problem solving (29). In some instances teacher interaction in the form of crisis intervention may be necessary to prevent a disaster, but even then students need to be encouraged to form self-management skills. Additional facets of the planning process include identifying behaviors and contexts that need to be altered if the student is to successfully resolve the stress, developing a scheme by which to achieve desired changes, locating resources that the student can use in the stress-resolution process, and organizing a system by which the student can acquire feedback on her or his progress in dealing with the problem (25). A critical part of any plan to resolve negative stress is the support system available to students as they attempt to resolve their concerns. Peer support groups, counseling sessions, and parent-teacher support efforts are effective ways of guiding students toward handling stress in positive ways (57, 62, 82). In severe cases of student stress, teachers should involve mental health professionals as soon as possible.

Carrying out plans to resolve student stress requires consistent action on the part of the teacher. This is especially true if the teacher's behavior is a major cause of the stress. Questions such as the following are helpful during the implementation process:

1. Is the student implementing changes to deal with the identified stress?

2. As a teacher am I carrying out supportive actions to assist the student in resolving stress?

3. If the peer group is a part of the plan, are the members responding productively to their role in the stress-resolution process?

4. Are indicators emerging that signal improvement in the student's ability to interact in the classroom, at home, or in the community?

5. If the plan is not working, has some action been taken to regroup and develop some alternative strategies for resolving the stress?

The resolution of any stress-inducing situation should be approached as a learning experience. Students need to experience success in solving problems and to acquire the skills that will enable them to persist until they do achieve such success. When they have succeeded, students need reinforcement to build on the success; when they fail, they need guidance on how to explore new ways of dealing with the situation (67). The *monitoring of student behavior* is linked to their continued growth, even after the stress has been resolved. Providing students with continued guidance can help them deal proactively with future problems. The stress-resolution process is never complete, and teacher actions to promote student competence in dealing with various life issues should be an integral part of the instructional focus (7).

EXTENSION STRATEGIES

The prevention and resolution of a great deal of classroom stress involve efforts to reach out to parents and citizens, to educate and involve them in changing many practices that are causing student stress (39, 48, 54). Strategies to extend the educators' reach to involve parents and citizens in the prevention and resolution of unhealthy stress are explored in the final section of this chapter.

Involving Parents in Stress Prevention

Parents should play a major role in the stress-prevention process. Strategies for involving them in this process include educating them about the importance of healthy family life; providing them with information on appropriate expectations for their child's developmental status; encouraging them to develop and maintain positive relationships with their child; providing them with information on causes, symptoms, and resolutions related to stress in children and adolescents; and educating them about strategies they can use to prevent or resolve stress-related issues (7, 9, 19, 37, 40, 50, 62, 69, 82, 84).

Productive family life has been documented as a major stress-prevention variable (9). Providing parents with early and continuing education about the characteristics of quality family life is a technique that many schools are using successfully to prevent unhealthy stress from emerging in students. Seminars, newsletter reminders, home visit programs, and other means of disseminating information to parents are focusing on the following as core awareness items: communication is a key indicator of healthy families, spending time together in family activities builds security and confidence in children and adolescents, and the sharing of family jobs strengthens everyone's commitment to the family (9). Students who have extreme difficulties with stress are typically portrayed as lacking healthy family dynamics. The many demands of modern living make it essential for parents to understand the importance of this process as it relates to the healthy development of children and adolescents.

A major source of stress in students is the parental expectation that they perform at levels inappropriate for their stage of development (19, 20). For example, many preschool children are asked to adjust to social and "academic" contexts that they are unprepared to cope with in a reasonable manner. As a result, children fail to develop positive behaviors for responding to group situations and often develop mental health problems (19). In the same way, many adolescents are thrust into adult situations too early and end up confused, anxious, and, in some cases, impotent in the face of unrealistic challenges (20). While many parents face an almost impossible task of meeting work and family demands, it is vital that they receive information on developmentally appropriate experiences for their children. Further, teachers and other helping professionals should provide parents with strategies and resources to use in carrying out the needed activities related to children's healthy functioning (9, 20, 76, 84). Figure 10 provides a basic list of items to share with parents on the issue of what is developmentally appropriate for children and adolescents.

Continuing, positive interaction between parents and children is linked to the prevention and resolution of student stress (9, 76). Reading together, sharing recreational activities, discussing common concerns, attending school events together, and scheduling special times for each other are ways in which to build this positive parent-child relationship (84). It is important for parents to realize that from the very beginning of family life, these relationships are being formed. In recent years many educators have advocated and implemented parenting programs for new parents, and the results have been encouraging. Research from these programs indicates that knowledgeable parents are having a positive influence on their children's development and learning (9, 10, 19). Two National Education Association publications that are useful for parents and teachers in carrying out such programs are *Parenting* and *Parents and Teachers as Discipline Shapers* (see Additional Readings).

Every family confronts at least some severe stress during the life cycle. Parents need to have information about the major sources of stress, stress symptoms, and strategies and resources to use to resolve unhealthy stress. Questions such as the following can be used as the basis for a series of seminars for parents:

1. What are the major sources of stress during early childhood, middle childhood, preadolescence, and adolescence?

2. How can I help my child to prevent stress?

3. How can I tell if my child is under intense stress?

4. What can I do to help a stressed child?

5. What can I be doing to prevent unhealthy stress from emerging in our family?

6. Once I know my child is a victim of stress, what are some strategies for resolving the situation?

Once again it is beneficial to involve parents in these seminars as early in the life of the family as feasible (9).

Figure 10
Parent Guidelines:
Developmentally Appropriate Experiences for Children

1. Children need a great deal of attention from adults, and especially from parents. Spend time with them and guide their development in positive directions.

2. Listen to your child's point of view, and respect his or her way of thinking. Remember, children are just beginning to construct their ideas of life, and they need many concrete, positive reinforcements on how to function.

3. Communicate often with your child's teacher. Share information you feel will help the teacher relate to your child in productive ways. Inquire about your child's total involvement in the classroom, and be supportive of the teacher.

4. Be sensitive to the fact that your child is "growing" and, thus, is not going to behave like an adult. Be patient, flexible, and helpful to your child in terms of this growth process.

5. Provide your child with clear, reasonable, and doable expectations for behavior; be firm but as positive as you can be in carrying out the discipline process.

6. Be a good example for your child. While no parent is perfect, parents can model sound nurturing and problem-solving behaviors.

7. Nurture a strong sense of warmth and humor in family interactions. Humor and warmth provide children and adults with some emotional common ground for developing their security and confidence.

8. Provide your child with many helping, caring experiences. Healthy children contribute to the well-being of other people.

9. Avoid placing your child in extremely stressful situations and try to avoid such predicaments yourself.

10. Maintain a continuing interest in your child's development. When you notice unusual behavior, find out what is happening in your child's world.

Another extension effort that is essential to resolving the many stressors that influence students is the involvement of community leaders and citizens in the shaping of healthy and productive environments.

Families and schools must function within the larger society. Indeed, stress that is created by community action or inaction is a major factor in student-related problems. For example, inadequate day care programs cause stress in children and parents, and this, in turn, often leads to poor social behaviors that the child then uses in later school involvement (76). Another indicator of community-centered stress is the lack of meaningful "passages" for adolescents and young adults to use in making their way into the adult world (10). Additional stressors that directly or indirectly influence students negatively include excessive work demands on parents, an insensitivity to parent needs related to family life, a lack of community supports for students and parents, and an inadequate system for nurturing student interests and talents (3).

Strategies to involve the total community in preventing and resolving stress-inducing elements include the following:

1. Sponsoring awareness events that raise the community's consciousness about stressors that can be prevented or resolved through community action. For example, one community has reduced drug usage among children and adolescents through its many drug awareness projects.

2. Involving community leaders of many orientations as resource people to deal with student stressors that can be resolved through a school-community partnership.

3. Teaming with parents to bring about changes in the community that are essential to improving the conditions under which parents carry out their parenting role. For example, parent-teacher groups have formed partnerships to press for improved after-school programs, summer employment projects, community fine arts activities, and many other endeavors.

4. Forming an "adopt a school" program with business and industry that fosters linkages between school and work that are meaningful to students. Involved students rarely suffer from negative stress.

5. Involving students in community leadership roles in which they can see the positive effects of their participation in projects to improve the quality of life. For example, students can write letters to the newspaper, serve as liaisons on community boards, carry out clean-up projects, and create community awareness of needs that require attention.

Ultimately, the current epidemic of stress-related problems that are impeding the lives of students demands the attention of every citizen. Teachers can play a major role in resolving the stress symptoms by carrying out prevention and resolution strategies in their classrooms, by involving parents in educational programs designed to promote positive student functioning, and by providing leadership in the community to foster improved conditions for families and schools. It would be foolish to limit stress-resolution efforts to any one dimension of the human ecology. What is needed is a renaissance of all human elements in the community that focuses on the recognition and use of the talents of children and young people.

Chapter 5
A SYSTEMS APPROACH FOR DEALING WITH CLASSROOM STRESS

Teachers who handle classroom stress effectively are dealing with many dimensions of stress in a systemic way. They do not adhere rigidly to a system but use it as a means of creating a viable management system—one that is based on student involvement, teacher invention, and student-teacher interactions that reflect mutual respect and sensitivity to their common and unique needs. Successful ventures in classroom management are characterized by an orderly, but open approach to dealing with human behavior. This chapter presents teachers with a mindful approach to use in dealing with classroom stress. Before articulating a systems design for dealing with classroom stress, the basic paradigms of systems theory are examined and some key insights on the many aspects of classroom stress are explicated. These two sections of the chapter serve as a foundation for the systems approach described in the last section.

BASIC PARADIGMS OF THE SYSTEMS APPROACH

In contrast to the reductionist approach of analyzing behavior in terms of a singular cause, the systemic-ecological perspective attempts to grasp as much of the total context of behavior as is humanly possible (5). For example, while a student may be under stress because of peer pressure, it is unlikely that this is her or his sole source of anxiety. Systems theorists would say that it is more likely that there are several factors interacting in the life of the student to stimulate such great stress. Indeed, there is some evidence to suggest that people use certain elements in their environment to counterbalance stressors and, thus, return their "system" to some form of equilibrium (30). It appears that severe negative behavioral patterns emerge only when several elements in a person's ecology are stressed. Further, the "system" each individual brings to interactions with other systems is an important factor in stress formation.

Two features of systems theory provide a foundation for examining classroom stress: (1) the individual is viewed as the primary unit of the human system, and (2) all human behavior is believed to proceed according to some system that has a structure and a process to it (64). When studying any system, such as the family or the classroom, one must eventually focus on the individual as the basic element in the system. Failing to recognize and utilize individual behaviors as a source of information when designing classroom management strategies will doom the resulting plan to failure. The physical, social, cognitive, and emotional composite of each student is what makes it possible to have a human system such as the classroom (29). Likewise, the behavior of each student in the classroom has "purpose" to it. Even when certain patterns of behavior may not coincide with accepted practice, the deviant pattern clearly meets some individual criterion of purpose. For example, while attention-getting behavior does not correspond with desired classroom behavior, it does meet the student's goal of receiving validation (30). Thus, an initial guideline for dealing with classroom stress is to know the patterns of individual student behaviors and as much as possible about the function of these behaviors (7).

A third feature of systems theory is that any system is comprised of all of the elements that combine to provide the identity essential to being called a system. For example, in a classroom the students, teacher, textbooks, physical setting, time schedules, resources, interpersonal relationships, and a myriad of other elements combine to form the physical, social, and psychological boundaries of this system (5). The unique way in which these elements interact influences any particular classroom to become what it is in terms of a social identity. Any attempt to "reduce" the elements of the classroom system will distort the total picture and, thus, provide a faulty perception of what is taking place (3, 37).

A fourth component of systems theory is the notion that every system is comprised of subsystems and interacts with these subsystems as well as with suprasystems (10). Subsystems might include cliques within the classroom, grouping schemes devised by the teacher, and nonverbal social units that form as a result of teacher-designed instructional activities. Suprasystems would include school policies, district directives, state education mandates, community expectations, and family values (39). It is clear that classrooms do function within other systems and do act as system influencers to others. What does or does not happen can cause much stress internally and in other systems.

This leads us to yet a fifth feature of systems theory: whatever happens in one system influences all other systems in some manner. An extension of this concept is that any change within a system influences all elements of the system (10). This is shown in the following example:

Edward is under great pressure at home and takes out his anxiety by constantly disrupting class. The disruptions influence other students in negative ways and soon the teacher is responding with punitive measures. Many parents complain because their children are disenchanted and then the principal asks to see the teacher.

69

While not every case is this severe, it does illustrate how any single incident can have multiple influences on other elements in that system and on other systems (3). Stress research results confirm that when any human system becomes engrossed in multiple stress patterns, everyone in the system is victimized in some way and is likely to carry the stress to other systems (48). The interactional nature of stress as it occurs in classroom systems is depicted in Figure 11.

Figure 11
The Interactional Nature of Classroom Stress

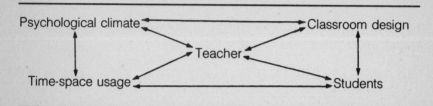

Systems theory is also supported in terms of the notion that any system must function in relation to other systems. For example, the classroom is linked to the school, is connected intimately to families, and is certainly an inherent part of the broader societal system. Research reports that low parental support of the teacher and the educational process negatively influences students (8). Likewise, evidence suggests that "inviting" schools (schools in which classrooms welcome parents and actively engage them in the educational process) prompt healthy functioning in children and adults (67). Figure 12 depicts the interactional process of classrooms with other systems.

It is clear that as a human system, the classroom has a high stress potential. Because it is embedded in the center of all social activity, many stress sources impinge on it, and it has the power to influence many systems in negative or positive ways. Thus, the problem-free classroom is more a dream than a reality. In fact, a classroom that is too quiet might reflect many hidden stressors rather than being a model place for learning (7).

Using data generated from research on classroom systems, the following suggestions provide a foundation for initiating stress-prevention and -resolution strategies:

1. Healthy systems are characterized as having secure and capable individuals. Thus, a cornerstone of stress-prevention/resolution strategies is nurturing the development of competence in each student (61).

70

Figure 12
Interaction of the Classroom with Other Systems

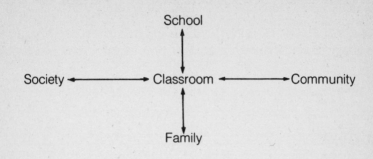

2. Human systems that produce high-quality outcomes are often described as places in which people function in cooperative, harmonious, and supportive ways. Thus, utilize cooperative learning strategies that stimulate meaningful, positive interactions among all students (14, 53).

3. Systems that incorporate feedback arrangements into their design respond to change in a viable way. Thus, interact with students, observe classroom happenings, and use other feedback devices such as parent conferences to refine and improve the classroom system (5, 7, 77).

4. Systems that have a "mission" tend to generate a sense of group identity that provides a framework in which individuals can develop their unique talents. Thus, have a clear purpose for the instructional program and involve students in activities in which they can contribute to this function (77).

5. Healthy systems develop and maintain productive relationships with other systems that are a part of their ecology. Thus, involve parents, citizens, and other community resource people in the classroom program (77).

6. Systems that have strong, yet sensitive leadership prove to be self-renewing and growth-oriented. Thus, utilize proactive behaviors such as planning effectively, fostering positive interpersonal behaviors, and developing active listening skills to provide the classroom with sound leadership (67).

7. Human systems depend on input from the participants for growth and productive development. Thus, design the classroom so as to

involve students in all facets of the program (77).

8. Systems have (or develop) limits within which productive functioning is possible; when these limits are exceeded by too many demands, the potential for unhealthy stress is increased. Thus, monitor the human equilibrium of the classroom so corrective action can be taken if the group stability is threatened (5, 7).

9. Communication among participants is essential to the development of internal and external linkages that provide human systems with the substance of identity. Thus, foster many positive interpersonal relationships in the classroom (18).

10. Evaluation of "system functioning" has proved to be vital to assuring the renewal of the system. Thus, take stock of the classroom ecology in terms of human dimensions as well as the more traditional assessments (31).

A systemic view of classroom stress provides teachers with a perceptual tool for conducting prevention/resolution actions that focus on maximizing the human potential of each student. In this paradigm, classroom events are seen as interrelated, purposeful, and—very importantly—improvable.

KNOWING THE MANY ASPECTS OF STRESS

Stress is such a complex process that it is impossible to fully grasp its totality. However, research has produced some insights that can serve as guidelines in responding to stress as it occurs in the classroom. And, in fact, in order to systematically study classroom stress, the many dimensions of this issue must be understood as much as possible.

The following are key points that research has generated regarding the various dimensions of stress:

1. Stress exists when both a stressor and a response are present. Stress represents a disruption in an individual's equilibrium. This disruption may be caused by negative or positive changes in the individual's life (7).

2. Stress is a perceptual event in that the existence of a stressor depends on the individual's perception of it as being disruptive to his or her system (44).

3. Stress is holistic in that it affects all elements of the person's system and has the potential to influence other people and other systems (64).

4. While stress may begin with the individual, if enough people develop similar perceptions, it can become a group process (7).

5. Stress can be categorized as either *acute* or *chronic*. Acute stressors are usually short in duration, often disappearing as rapidly as they emerge. Chronic stress usually evolves more slowly but is cumulative in nature and potentially more damaging because it has more time to erode the human system (7, 19).

6. Stress is context-induced and related to specific stages of life. For example, teachers often cite these student-related stressors in the school: tests, teacher behavior, peer pressure, academic pressure, classroom climate, and crowded classrooms (7).

7. Stress is not always an observable event. In some cases people hide their stress, letting it gather force and become a significant part of their lives. This is sometimes viewed as a form of a "mental time bomb" because the results of stress must eventually be dealt with in some manner (19, 20, 21).

8. Stress is a learned process, and, thus, the experiences people have with stress shape their pattern of responding to it. For example, students who fear new situations to an unusual degree have usually acquired this fear as a result of interactions with significant others and/or the environment (58).

9. Stress can be managed, and proactive strategies are the most effective because they provide the individual with some anticipatory control over her or his setting. Finding out what stressors have the most negative influence on oneself and then forming strategies to control these stressors is an effective way of reducing stress (44).

10. Uncontrolled stress that permeates an individual's life system can lead to burnout. When burnout occurs, intensive therapy is usually needed to enable the individual to revive his or her control system (64).

When teachers understand the dimensions of the stress process, they have the information essential to making critical judgments about student behavior in classroom settings. The stress-management system described in the next section of this chapter should be used as a guide. Avoid adhering to it in a rigid manner, and utilize mental health professionals in stress cases that are clearly beyond the realm of normal functioning.

A SYSTEM FOR DEALING WITH CLASSROOM STRESS

The systems framework for managing classroom stress is depicted in Figure 13. It includes three major components: assessing the classroom ecology, formulating a plan of action, and creating a productive classroom ecology. These components interface with each other, influencing what happens or can happen in the total classroom system. For example, effective planning is dependent on the results obtained during the assessment process, and in order to carry out assessment, a viable classroom management system must be in operation.

Figure 13
A System for Dealing with Classroom Stress

ASSESSING THE CLASSROOM ECOLOGY

Developing the planning framework
Establishing assessment categories
Interpreting the data
Utilizing the findings

FORMULATING A PLAN OF ACTION

Articulating specific needs
Developing goals and objectives
Identifying strategies and resources
Deploying an implementation design
Assessing results

CREATING A PRODUCTIVE CLASSROOM ECOLOGY

Ensuring quality teacher behaviors
Creating dynamic program direction
Developing a caring classroom
Involving parents and citizens

It should also be noted that like any system, it should be used to meet student needs and not adhered to in a rigid manner. In other words, teachers may find themselves using all three components simultaneously in order to deal with a particular classroom situation. The intent of any systemic framework is that it be used in a viable manner. Thus, the following presentation on the components of the system is intended as a guide on how to use it, and not as a sequential process that must be followed rigidly.

Assessing the Classroom Ecology

Four elements combine to make up the ecological assessment process: developing the planning framework, establishing assessment categories, formulating guidelines to use in interpreting the data gathered, and determining ways to use the data. These elements of the assessment process can be used in a simplified manner or can become the foundation for an elaborate study of classroom stress.

Developing the Planning Framework

Whom to Involve: Any design to assess classroom stress begins with the people conducting it. The parameters of the project will often dictate who should be involved. For example, if the purpose is to acquire a general picture of the classroom climate, the teacher may decide to handle the project alone or to involve only one or two other teachers. This type of effort is often termed a *preliminary assessment approach*. If the function of the study to to carry out an in-depth analysis of stress in terms of individual students and/or group behaviors, it would be advisable to form a planning team similar to those used in curriculum studies. The team would consist of the teacher, some parents, student representatives when appropriate, possibly the school counselor, and other professional staff as needed.

How to Conduct the Study: The mechanics of carrying out an assessment of classroom stress will vary according to the functions of identified studies. Large-scale studies on stress include the following: specified functions of the study, a time line for the achievement of each function, valid data-gathering devices, task lists for each study team member, and some process for monitoring the progress made during the study. The advantage of having a planned process to use in carrying out studies on classroom stress is that people have a clear direction and a system by which to pursue their goals. While sporadic efforts to resolve stress situations may prove useful, without a systematic approach a great deal of insight is often lost. Providing direction to the who, how, when, and where of classroom stress assessments increases the likelihood of useful results.

How to Gather Data on Stress: There are various ways to gather data on classroom stress: teacher observation, inventories and questionnaires, interviews with students and/or parents, "classroom climate" checklists,

75

and analysis of student histories. Many teachers use these techniques informally and as a part of their daily instructional activities. Yet, results from studies using a systems approach point out that a more formalized and planned use of these devices yields more reliable data, which, in turn, provides a solid foundation for resolving the problem (7).

When the time arrives to carry out the assessment process, some questions that relate to the foundation of the plan must be asked:

1. Has a specific function for the study been determined?

2. Has a planning team been formed? Are the team members informed regarding the purpose of the study? Have they completed their preparation tasks so that the study can be conducted effectively?

3. Has a time line of tasks to be completed been developed to provide direction to the work of the study team?

4. Have data-gathering procedures been selected and/or developed for use in carrying out the functions of the study?

5. Has a person/process been established for monitoring the progress of the study?

Establishing Assessment Categories

A second element of the assessment process is the determination of what to assess in terms of classroom stress. Four categories of classroom stress provide the framework for this process: teacher behaviors, the classroom ecology, student behaviors, and extra-classroom stressors.

Teacher as Stressor: It has been determined that teachers can be a significant source of stress for students (55, 78). A common scenario is that of the stressed teacher injecting her or his stress into the events of the classroom. Unfortunately, teachers suffering from chronic stress rarely see themselves as a possible stressor. Key teacher behaviors to examine include classroom management skills, instructional competence, attitudes toward students and parents, involvement in personal and professional growth activities, and the overall emotional orientation (18, 38, 77, 78). Techniques for assessing teachers' stress orientation include completing self-assessment checklists (see *Stress and the Classroom Teacher* [78]), videotaping selected segments of the teacher's workday, using peer teachers to study the classroom, and interviewing students and parents on the teacher's functioning. Teacher assessment should be handled in a productive manner; the individual teacher should be a part of the process and the purpose should be to use the feedback gained to improve the classroom situation.

The Classroom Ecology—What to Study: Research on classroom-induced stress provides several clues as to what to examine in the classroom context (18). One observation has been that involved, active students tend to be a reflection of the curriculum orientation. Narrowly focused instructional programs seem to create stress because only a few students can find meaning in such an arrangement (7). The following findings provide a starting point for analyzing the classroom in terms of its stress potential:

1. An excessively authoritarian attitude exists in the classroom. A threatening atmosphere induces excessive stress in students (34).

2. Punishment is given unfairly, harshly, and without relationship to the severity of the offense. Punitive environments increase the stress potential in students (7).

3. The time management scheme is rigid and/or poorly organized. Rigidity and/or chaos induces a great deal of unhealthy stress (33).

4. The classroom is too crowded or space is poorly planned, thus leaving students with few opportunities to engage in active learning. A closed-in feeling is related to student stress (77).

5. The social climate is one of alienation; students have few opportunities to work together or to participate in the management of the classroom (67).

6. The instructional program is limited and does not reflect student interests and talents (77).

Blom, Cheney, and Snoddy (7) add to this list excessive testing, inordinate academic pressure, poor human relationships, ineffective family-school relationships, and unhealthy levels of competition. Assessments of classroom settings indicate that when several of these indicators exist in the environment, the potential for student stress becomes quite high (10, 67, 77). For an elaboration of items related to classroom-induced stress, see *A Proactive Approach to Discipline* (77) and *Maintaining Productive Student Behavior* (listed in Additional Readings).

Student-Induced Stress: Each student defines what is stressful in terms of a history of life experiences. The physical, social, cognitive, and emotional make-up of students influences their behavior. For example, poor nutrition can impede an individual's system, thus causing stress in all facets of life (54, 60). Likewise, deficits in cognitive processing may lead to academic frustrations, thus prompting a series of stress reactions. Student behavior patterns to watch for during stress analysis include the following:

1. Poor eating and sleeping habits

2. Student isolation from routine classroom events

3. Continued poor academic performance

4. Constant complaining, cynical attitudes, and related indicators of defeatism

5. Excessive aggression or unwarranted tantrums and other related antisocial acts

6. Unusual and marked changes in typical behavior patterns.

In addition to individual student stress, it is important to watch for stress reactions in the total class group. For example, the death of a classmate is likely to stress the entire class. Teachers must be aware of student reactions to tragic or threatening events if they want to handle these issues in a productive way (77).

Beyond the Classroom—Common Student Stressors: One of the tenets of systems theory that is obvious to students of classroom stress is that human systems are interrelated, and whatever happens in one system influences all other connected systems (10). When a child experiences dramatic change at home or lives in fear because of an unsafe neighborhood, he or she is likely to transfer those anxieties to the classroom context (3, 27, 77). The following are the most common stressors to look for during stress analysis: death of a parent, loss of a sibling, divorce, parents on drugs, peer pressure to use drugs, initial entrance into foster family care, stepfamily formation, conflict in the family or neighborhood, latchkey status, alcoholism in the family or an alcoholic peer, child abuse and neglect, and unrealistic expectations by parents. There are additional stressors such as poverty, work overload, and others that are insidious to social status. Teachers can watch for these "beyond the classroom" stressors by staying directly involved with students and maintaining continued communication with parents (7).

Interpreting the Data

Once data has been gathered on classroom stress, the method used to interpret it is vital to forming a workable resolution. While teacher observation is often a reliable way of determining what is happening in the classroom, many student behaviors carry multiple messages—that is, they present several messages at one time. For example, a student's failure to complete schoolwork may mean that he is having a problem at home, is upset over a peer problem, is unable to do the assignment, or has some other problem. Thus, it is important to study one's observations to validate or refute what first appears to be obvious. The use of selected student behavior inventories, informal interviews with students, and parent conferences will help teachers acquire a clear picture of what student behaviors mean (77).

Many stress researchers advocate a team approach to studying school and classroom stress. A team of teachers, the school counselor, parent representatives, and students can combine their efforts to analyze possible stress sources in or connected to the school ecology (7). This approach is certainly necessary when looking at group stress that may be linked to several complex sources. It is also beneficial when analyzing a student who may have a complex history of socioemotional maladies. For example, school-community teams that have successfully studied stressors related to student drug usage point to the broad insights obtained by involving many different constituencies in their work.

Any data on student stress must be related to the "big picture" of how the student functions in various settings. These questions require answers during the data analysis process: Is the stress exhibited by the student in the classroom related to her or his functioning at home? Is the stress situation temporary and, thus, resolvable with minor adjustments? Is the stress related to developmental changes or to an ecological change such as moving to a new community? These and additional questions can place particular stress situations into the larger context.

Utilizing the Findings

The final element in the assessment process is the determination of how to utilize the findings of your analysis. Following are five common outcomes that emerge from classroom stress studies:

Refine Teacher Behaviors: Assessment results may indicate that certain teacher behavior is causing student stress and, thus, warrants study and refinement (78). For example, Purkey and Novak (67) note that many teachers unknowingly alienate students from the mainstream of events by failing to involve them in learning activities or by branding them as discipline problems. Behaviors that need continual attention are attitudes toward students, nonverbal interaction patterns, student assessment strategies, verbal teaching style, and behaviors related to the teacher's professional and personal development (8, 66). The ability to refine and/or alter certain teacher behaviors in light of feedback from students or peers is indicative of a capable, developing teacher.

Refine Student Behaviors: Since stress is an individually defined process, in many cases some form of student behavioral change will be required. Individuals develop patterns of responding to stressors, and while it may be possible to eliminate some stress from the environment, in some situations the student will have to alter his or her perceptual-behavioral orientation (40). A typical example is the child who is experiencing anxiety over going to school for the first time. Since school is a requirement in our society, the child will have to learn to deal with it in some functional way. With support from parents and teachers, children usually refine their orientation to school in a positive manner. Strategies that appear to facilitate students in their coping with stress include teaching problem-solving skills, involving them in empathetic listening activities, counseling them informally, and encouraging them to develop positive attitudes toward self and others (9, 28). A note of caution is in order: some students have severe problems and require sophisticated intervention by a qualified mental health professional.

Refine Parent Behaviors: Recent national assessments of stress in children and adolescents indicate parents need to rethink their role in the human development process (see "Children Under Stress," cited in the Additional Readings section of this book). The data indicates that children need parents to perform more of a nurturing, buffer role because of the increasing complexity of choices and challenges they face at school, in the neighborhood, and in the community at large. However, it appears that for an increasing number of children, the typical life experience is loneliness, artifical pressure to grow up too fast, and little emotional support for dealing with their childhood as a developmental experience (19, 20, 21).

Assessments indicate the following to be the most common parent stressors:

1. Excessive absence from the home, which is the primary setting for parent-child interaction (10).

2. Pressure (often in culturally accepted forms) for the child to become an adult and, thus, bypass the formative stage of childhood (63, 65).

3. Failure to guide the child's development, thus exposing the child to the risks of excessive television watching and/or the vagaries of the peer group (20).

4. Unrealistic expectations in terms of the child's academic achievement, which then becomes a source of further stress in the parent-child relationship (21).

5. Severe neglect and/or abuse of the child in terms of basic human needs. Children who are victims of this "cipher syndrome" often exhibit severe stress symptoms, if not in childhood, certainly by adolescence and young adulthood (13).

Refinements in parental behavior can be achieved through direct counseling and parent intervention programs, and through indirect efforts with church groups, civic projects, and interdisciplinary professional teams. An important extension of this support process is to provide parents with tools to change their context, thus freeing them to perform parenting roles that are critical to having healthy children and adolescents.

Refine the Classroom Ecology: Classroom stress-analysis studies often reveal the need for change in the environment. Certainly there are constraints on what teachers can alter and limits within which they can attempt to improve their situation. Yet, many teachers have found ways to reduce classroom stress by creating options within a particular environment. For example, a teacher might not be able to enlarge the classroom, but she or he can improve the situation by refining the way in which the existing space is used. Typical stressors that can be altered are time management, space usage, student grouping patterns, the psychological climate of the classroom, and student seating arrangements. In many cases, minor adjustments in the environment can resolve student stress (77).

Refine the Curriculum: A curriculum devoid of meaning is certain to prompt student stress. Unfortunately, many curriculum studies simply calculate the "content" value of material being taught. A comprehensive study of curricular designs should probe the total arrangement: materials, instructional strategies, goals, resources, assessment procedures, individuation of content for special student needs, and other pertinent items. Narrowly defined and pedantic instructional programs stunt the student's learning and increase his or her stress level (77).

The culmination of the assessment process should be to pull together the major needs identified for application in the plan of action.

Formulating a Plan of Action

Now that we have identified the problems, what can we do to resolve the situation? The formulation of a viable plan of action involves five components: articulating specific needs, developing goals and objectives, identifying strategies and resources, deploying an implementation design, and assessing the results of the plan.

Articulating Specific Needs

Each classroom stress study will identify unique needs. The articulation of these needs is the first component of the planning process. An effective way to categorize needs is to use the assessment findings relative to the key areas of teacher behaviors, student behaviors, parent behaviors, classroom ecology, curriculum, and extra-classroom elements.

Examples of needs that have been identified by teachers during their stress assessments are as follows:

- *Teacher Behavior Need:* Spend more time with Albert and Jonita, especially as related to their feelings about classroom activities.

- *Student Behavior Need:* John needs more support in building his self-image; his self-derogation seems endless and implies a need for major intervention.

- *Parent Behavior Need:* Parents are pushing their children too much and need educational ideas on appropriate expectations for children at different stages of development.

- *Classroom Ecology Need:* Space is at a premium, and a need exists to reorganize the physical structure of the room.

- *Curriculum Revision Need:* Students are doing too much seatwork and need to be involved in projects that challenge them.

- *Other Needs:* The community is too isolated from the school; community people need to be involved as resource teachers in the classroom on a regular basis.

Developing Goals and Objectives

Emerging from the needs-articulation process is the foundation of any plan: the goals and objectives related to resolving and/or preventing classroom stressors. Most plans establish broad goals that provide overall direction. Specific objectives are then identified in a priority manner within a long-range/short range framework.

It is important to remember when developing any planning framework to combat classroom stress that the dynamic nature of living systems like classrooms requires the flexible handling and continual revision of such tools (77). Events in the classroom, at home, or in the life of the teacher may prompt refinement or revision of stress-management plans. Given this cautionary note about utilizing goal/objective frameworks as "guides" to be manipulated in relation to the ecological changes of the classroom, the following is a sample of such a framework:

GOAL 1: To implement parent education strategies that provide parents with information on appropriate expectations for children in the primary grades. The intent is to awaken parents to the fact that many children are stressed by unreal parental expectations.

GOAL 2: *Short-Range Objective:* To conduct a workshop on "Stress and Young Children" for parents of children in the primary grades. The program will be conducted early in the school year. The focus will be on specific things parents can do to reduce negative stress in their children.

Long-Range Objective: To develop and implement a stress-prevention program for parents of preschool-age children. The program will be developed this school year and piloted during the next school year. The focus will be on reaching first-time parents with information on how to develop healthy relationships with their children, thus reducing the probability of stress in the child's life.

GOAL 2. To reconstruct the time and space usage plan for the classroom. The intent is to experiment with a less rigid arrangement that may allow students to progress in a more functional manner.

Short-Range Objective: To re-do the time schedule of daily activities to give students more opportunities to make transitions from one learning situation to another and to integrate what they have learned into their planning for the next day.

Long-Range Objective: To design some alternative space usage plans for experimental use during the next school year. At least three plans will be developed for this project.

Identifying Strategies and Resources

To achieve the desired goals and objectives, usable strategies and resources must be identified and prepared for the classroom. Analysis of the goals/objectives area will provide key indicators for meeting this planning need. For example, plans that focus on parent education may require specific materials, resource people skilled in helping parents, appropriate films, and other parent training materials. Efforts to refine the classroom ecology will have a different set of needs: in-service education programs on classroom management, visits to other classrooms, consultants who are skilled in time management, and other appropriate resources. One way to organize the process of obtaining needed resources and of designing and/or selecting viable strategies is to categorize them in the following areas: student development strategy/resource needs, parent development strategy/resource needs, classroom development strategy/resource needs, curriculum development strategy/resource needs, and extra-classroom development strategy/resource needs.

Deploying an Implementation Design

The implementation of stress-prevention/resolution plans can be facilitated by incorporating the following steps into the planning process:

1. Develop a time line that specifies desired dates for carrying out various features of the plan. A task completion chart such as the following is a helpful reminder to everyone about the who, what, when, and where components of the plan:

Objective	Completion date	Activity	Responsible party	Location

2. Monitor the implementation of new activities or schedules in the classroom; changes require intentional effort on the part of everyone involved. For example, if a student has contracted to carry out certain tasks, be sure to check on her or his progress on a daily or weekly basis.

3. Utilize a team approach; stress management usually requires the cooperation of several parties to alter the situations that prompted stress. Class meetings, counseling with parents, teacher teams, and peer support groups are some examples of this cooperative process.

4. Develop and maintain a sense of optimism about the ultimate success of your plan. A positive attitude is infectious in that others begin to believe in themselves as a result of your proactive orientation. When certain techniques fail, show students how to reassess the situation and replan need strategies.

5. Integrate into your implementation activities as many self-management strategies as possible. The ultimate goal of stress-management programs is to have students and teachers acquire autonomy in handling a variety of problem-solving strategies in a proactive manner.

Assessing the Results

Determining the success of a stress-management program is a multifaceted process. Questions such as the following provide a foundation for carrying out this process:

1. What were your original criteria for success? What goals and objectives were defined at the outset of the program?

2. If a team approach was used, did people follow through on assigned tasks? How well did they do in carrying out the various assignments? What improvements or refinements can be made in future efforts?

3. During implementation, were adjustments made that altered the initial focus of the program? If so, how does this influence the assessment process?

4. List the different stress-management strategies used and record some observations you made regarding the utility of each strategy. Did these strategies facilitate or impede your efforts?

5. Has the stress situation in the classroom been improved as a result of your efforts? If not, why not? Where did the process fail, and how can it be refined or altered within a new plan?

The evaluation of stress-prevention/resolution efforts must be viewed as a continuing process, one that uses feedback to refine practices and to provide direction for new efforts. The ultimate goal of this assessment process should be to focus on how teachers, students, and parents are dealing with stress. That is, are people beginning to take control of their behavior, perceive stressors as opportunities for creative problem solving, and utilize their experiences to build a proactive base that will prevent negative stress from becoming a major problem?

Creating a Productive Classroom Ecology

Beyond formative efforts to assess and resolve observable classroom stress problems is the power to promote maximum student development by creating a productive classroom ecology. Truly dynamic classrooms stimulate healthy stress in children and adolescents, and minimize the need for constant reactive efforts regarding stress management (61, 67, 75, 76, 84). A major finding of systems theory studies has been that in environments in which individuality and group functioning are integrated through diverse, supportive efforts, the functioning of the participants is heightened (3, 10).

Ensuring Quality Teacher Behaviors

Productive classroom ecologies appear to be the result of quality teaching. In spite of less than ideal conditions, many teachers have succeeded in constructing highly effective learning environments. Thus, this series of quality teacher behaviors represents the basis for creating healthy classroom settings:

1. Maintaining a healthy self-concept as a teacher and in one's personal life. Teachers who are positive about themselves, interested in new challenges, professionally active, and supportive of their peers are usually effective in relating to the totality of student needs (67).

2. Developing and nurturing many positive relationships with students. Take an active interest in their concerns, be a good listener, and support their proactive efforts to become self-managing individuals. Teachers who truly know their students through productive, warm interactions in the classroom are usually able to determine appropriate challenge levels for them. Students report that when they are challenged by sensitive, supportive teachers, they tend to respond positively (37, 77).

3. Maintaining a well-organized, well-managed classroom. Classrooms that have clear direction with plenty of chances for individuation are excellent stress-prevention settings. The students' ideal teacher is one who is able to organize a viable learning climate and, yet, accommodate the unique needs of different students (18, 84).

4. Integrating the affective learning of students into the basic instructional plan. Research reports that classrooms in which students are able to express their feelings, articulate their ideas, and develop their socioemotional selves have few major problems. Fairness, responsiveness, and nurturing are teacher behaviors that have been related to productive classroom designs (8, 10, 61).

5. Communicating with students and their parents on a continuing basis. Communication is the key to relationships, and helping students cope with stress requires that these relationships be authentic and linked to the environments in which development and learning are carried out (61, 67).

Creating Dynamic Program Direction

This teacher behavior deserves special attention. Boredom, confusion, irrelevance, and isolation are the roots of unhealthy stress. Programs that foster a sense of involvement, purpose, and vitality engage students in actions that will help them grow and develop. The following are indicators of dynamic learning programs that promote positive behavior in students:

1. Students receive a great deal of input through direct, concrete experiences. That is, students are challenged to use all of their senses in learning about ideas and events (34).

2. Students are involved in creating learning outcomes in many dimensions: visual creations, artistic expressions, story development, recordings, papers, plays, experiments, and related outcomes (77).

3. Students are able to progress as unique, important individuals and are encouraged to challenge themselves through a self-assessment process. The premise is that if individual students are progressing toward autonomy, the total group will become successful learners (75).

4. Students have access to a wide array of learning materials and experiences within a cooperative, sharing context. Student interests often prompt the introduction of new resources into the learning arrangement. It is common in such classrooms for student groups to pursue meaningful projects (14, 34).

5. Classroom learning is extended to "surrounding systems" through home learning, field trips, community resource people, and educational television. Students are encouraged to connect their learning to other settings through assignments, special projects, and parental guidance (10, 61, 84).

Nurturing a Caring Classroom

This teacher behavior also calls for emphasis because unhealthy stress is most likely to emerge in classrooms in which hostile, aggressive feelings are present. Children and adolescents who have a sense of ownership of the classroom usually channel their efforts in proactive directions. Ownership symbols include work displays, job assignments, student involvement in decision making, cooperative attitudes, teaming, and friendship (59, 67). Likewise, a sense of caring results when programs value the feelings of each person and set aside time to foster such caring. Classrooms in which students feel important, cared about, and connected to life's important events have little stress (10, 61).

Involving Parents and Citizens

Involving parents in the educational process is critical to having a healthy classroom system (77). A review of student stressors reveals that many of them reside in settings that are beyond the classroom (3, 69). For example, a great many of young children's problems in school have been linked to inadequate family dynamics (37). On a broader scale, local and global stressors often add to the discontinuity existent in the lives of students.

Beginning during the preschool years, parents should be educated about and involved in the prevention and resolution of negative stress. As a starting point, parents can be given information on the development of children, specific resources that they can use to build positive family relationships, and strategies that they can use to prevent unnecessary stress. An extension of this orientation is to make the parents active partners in planning and carrying out productive learning programs. Parents can serve in a variety of roles including tutors, storytellers, aides, and program leaders. A key feature of healthy ecologies is the intimate involvement of all the major participants in the human development process (7, 10, 24, 77).

Parents also need to be involved in specific stress-prevention/resolution plans. In many cases, parental leadership is required to resolve a stress. For example, if poor nutrition habits or lack of sleep is the source of stress, parents must participate in shaping a context that will prompt the desired student behavior changes. Parental involvement in specific stress-resolution plans can take many forms: acting as co-partner in the planning process, arranging home factors to support needed changes, monitoring the child's behavior, communicating with the teacher as needed, acquiring needed resources for the child, guiding the child toward more self-management roles, and acting as a resource person in the classroom (37, 77).

The community, both in the local sense and in the global perspective, needs attention in any program that focuses on improving student functioning. Local community involvement in dealing with issues that permeate the lives of children and adults can lead to desirable improvements in recreational outlets, mental health resources, community-centered literacy projects, and various other activities. In the "global community," many actions can have a positive influence on students: improvements in the quality of television programs, efforts to aid children in special situations such as those in poverty and/or war contexts, programs that focus on intercultural idea exchange, and awareness efforts related to human rights and human abuse. There is yet another dimension to this process: providing students with positive role models. Having community resource people share their expertise in problem solving and stress management is one way to provide such role models. Other possibilities include using community industries as learning laboratories, involving local leadership teams in family support efforts, using people in management roles as consultants on approaches to classroom management, and developing school-business partnerships that focus on building positive classroom learning settings (77).

THE CLASSROOM AS A DYNAMIC SYSTEM

The classroom is a dynamic set of human relationships, events, and ever-changing patterns that combine to make up a learning/development system. A systems approach to managing classroom stress must account for the living processes that occur in systems like classrooms. The components of the planning model presented in this chapter, for example, must be used in a flexible way, allowing feedback to alter and refine the plan as it is carried out. Feedback is the one feature of human systems that provides the power to shape and reshape behavior in light of new and/or emerging data. For example, new needs usually emerge as teachers come to know a student's situation. A student who originally appeared to be suffering only from poor sleeping habits may turn out to be experiencing emotional trauma at home. Or what appears to be a simple case of parent-child conflict may gradually unfold as a more complex family pathology. The dynamics of human systems offer the interested person a vast arena for creative study (32, 39, 76).

The changeability of a classroom system, as well as the viable nature of the systems surrounding and interacting with it, requires teachers to pursue stress management in a planned, but responsive manner. To synthesize some of the major points made in this book that relate to this planning orientation, five key areas are reviewed: teacher behavior, student behavior, classroom climate, curriculum, and stress influences that emanate from beyond the classroom.

Teacher behavior is the one variable that can be modified and refined in relation to stress-management actions. Given the research finding that productive teacher leadership strengthens the classroom ecology, this is a promising situation. *It is clear that teachers should avoid doing the following*:

- Inflicting negative attitudes on students
- Remaining isolated from students, peers, and parents
- Maintaining unreal and/or ill-founded expectations of students
- Using punitive discipline approaches that fail to support productive living in students
- Remaining static and uninvolved in personal and professional growth.

These behaviors produce stress because they usually degrade the student and eventually destroy the integrity of the teacher. *Fortunately, there are proactive teacher behaviors that have been related to positive developments in classrooms*:

- Maintaining a positive psychological orientation
- Continuing to grow and develop as a person and as a professsional
- Responding to student needs and concerns
- Experimenting with new ideas and challenges
- Interacting regularly with parent and students as well as with others connected to the classroom ecology
- Developing a dynamic learning program
- Promoting the total well-being of students (67, 77, 78).

Controlled, flexible, sensitive, and knowledgeable teachers are the keys to any viable stress-management plan.

Stressed students provide us with clues as to what is needed to nurture productive, healthy student behavior: a positive self-concept, problem-solving skills, a sense of optimism about the future, involvement in significant life events, support from parents and teachers, and the continuing development of socioeducational skills (2, 10, 25, 67, 77). *The key in studying student behavior is to look for dynamic patterns that are oriented toward positive, growing outcomes.* Developmental and personal shifts occur naturally on the life span continuum, especially when ecological changes take place as rapidly as they often do in contemporary society (22, 23, 24). The absence of proactive behavioral patterns or the existence of continued anxiety-ridden syndromes should prompt teachers and parents to probe the roots of student behavior. In the preventive vein, teachers can support student functioning by encouraging them to behave in caring, mindful, sensitive, and creative way (61, 76, 84).

The dynamics of the classroom climate are ultimately seen in the dimensions of the physical, social, and psychological actions of the participants. Classrooms are such complex arenas that no "model" exists that answers all of the important questions related to the development of fully functioning human beings. Rather, it is more of a what-to-do/what-not-to-do situation. For example, we know that rigid, boring, insensitive, noncooperative, unsupportive, and chaotic classrooms are major stress producers (77, 78). We also know that students need structure, space, time, a sense of validity, and opportunities to develop their socioemotional selves (24, 71). Thus, *the dynamic pattern to reach for is one that provides students with guidance and direction, and yet fosters in them the formation of self-management behaviors* (77).

Self-discipline is best acquired through learning experiences that strengthen decision-making and problem-solving skills (25). Stressed students are not able to proactively function in the environment. Constantly reacting to stress, many of these students develop fate-filled attitudes toward life and become very dependent on others to resolve their problems. Clearly, *the curriculum dynamics need to be designed to involve students in experiences that are challenging, developmentally appropriate, personally stimulating, and facilitative of their growth and development* (77).

This same construct applies to experiences that occur outside the classroom context. What happens in the home, in the neighborhood, and in the broader contexts of life now influences students as much as or more than what happens in the classroom. *Meaningful family life, linkages to the community, and opportunities to apply skills and talents in various contexts are essential to the full empowerment of children and adolescents.* The ultimate design for a healthy environment for students must reflect the positive direction that all adults participate in shaping—and this design must place first priority on human needs and the corresponding actions that match this vision.

BIBLIOGRAPHY

1. Abood, D. "The Plate-Spinner: A Stress Awareness Activity." *Health Education* 17, no. 4 (1986): 9.
2. Alschuler, A. *Teacher Burnout*. Washington, D.C.: National Education Association, 1984.
3. Apter, S. *Troubled Children/Troubled Systems*. New York: Pergamon Press, 1982.
4. Asher, S. "Some Kids Are Nobody's Best Friend." *Today's Education* 71 (1982): 22–29.
5. Benswager, E. "Stressful Events in Early Childhood Education: An Ecological Approach." *Child Care Quarterly* 11 (1982): 267–79.
6. Billings, A., and Moos, R. "Stressful Life Events and Symptoms: A Longitudinal Study." *Health Psychology* 1 (1982): 99–117.
7. Blom, G; Cheney, B.; and Snoddy, Jr. *Stress in Childhood: An Intervention Model for Teachers and Other Professionals*. New York: Teachers College Press, 1986.
8. Bloom, B. "Affective Outcomes of School Learning." *Phi Delta Kappan* 59, no 3 (1977): 193–98.
9. Brenner, A. *Helping Children Cope with Stress*. Lexington, Mass: D.C. Heath, 1984.
10. Bronfenbrenner, U. "Alienation and the Four Worlds of Childhood." *Phi Delta Kappan* 67, no. 6 (1986): 430–35.
11. Brown, B. "The Extent and Effects of Peer Pressure Among High School Students." *Journal of Youth and Adolescence* 11 (1982): 121–33.
12. Byrnes, D. "Forgotten Children in Classrooms: Development and Characteristics." *The Elementary School Journal* 84 (1984): 287–91.
13. ———. "Cipher in the Classroom." *Childhood Education* 62, no. 2 (1985): 91–97.
14. Cangelosi, J. *Cooperation in the Classroom: Students and Teachers Together*. Washington, D.C.: National Education Association, 1986.
15. Cook, J., and Cook, P. "Children in Crisis." *Early Years* 73 (1980): 73–74.
16. Cramer, W., and Dorsey, S. "Are Movers Losers?" *The Elementary School Journal* 70 (1970): 387–90.
17. Douglas, L. "Is Adolescent Suicide a Third Degree Game and Who Is the Real Victim?" *Transactional Analysis Journal* 16, no. 3 (1986): 161–64.
18. Duke, D. *Helping Teachers Manage Classrooms*. Alexandria, Va.: Association for Supervision and Curriculum Development, 1982.
19. Elkind, D. *The Hurried Child: Growing Up Too Fast, Too Soon*. Reading, Mass.: Addison-Wesley, 1981.
20. ———. *All Grown Up and No Place To Go*. Reading, Mass.: Addison-Wesley, 1981.
21. ———. "Stress and the Middle-Grader." *The School Counselor* 33 (1986): 196–206.

22. Erikson, E. *Identity and Youth Crisis*. New York: W.W. Norton, 1968.
23. _____. *Dimensions of a New Identity*. New York: W.W. Norton, 1974.
24. _____. *The Life Cycle Completed: A Review*. New York: W.W. Norton, 1982.
25. Etzioni, A. "The Role of Self-Discipline." *Phi Delta Kappan* 64, no. 3 (1982): 184–86.
26. Freeman, E. "When Children Face Divorce: Issues and Implications of Research." *Childhood Education* 62, no. 2 (1985): 130–36.
27. Frost, J. "Children in a Changing Society: Frontiers of Challenge." *Childhood Education* 62, no. 4 (1986): 242–49.
28. Gerler, E. "Skills for Adolescence: A New Program for Young Teenagers." *Phi Delta Kappan* 67, no. 6 (1986): 436–39.
29. Glasser, W. *Control Theory*. New York: Harper and Row, 1984.
30. Goldberger, L., and Breznitz, S. *Handbook of Stress: Theoretical and Clinical Aspects*. New York: The Free Press, 1982.
31. Goodal, R., and Brown, L. "The Development of an Instrument to Assess Classroom Climate." *The Journal of Classroom Interaction* 19, no. 1 (1983): 2–6.
32. Greenberg, H. *Coping with Job Stress*. Englewood Cliffs, N.J.: Prentice-Hall, 1980.
33. Hall, E. *The Dance of Life*. New York: Anchor Press/Doubleday, 1984.
34. Hart, L. *Human Brain and Human Learning*. New York: Longman, 1983.
35. Hetherington, M. "Divorce: A Child's Perspective." *American Psychologist* 34 (1979): 851–58.
36. Holzman, T. "Schools Can Provide Help for the Children of Divorce." *American School Board Journal* 171 (1984): 46–47.
37. Honig, A. "Stress and Coping in Children: Part I." *Young Children* 41, no. 4 (1986): 50–63.
38. _____. "Stress and Coping in Children: Part II." *Young Children* 41, no. 5 (1986): 47–59.
39. Humphrey, J., and Humphrey, J. *Controlling Stress in Children*. Springfield, Ill.: Charles C. Thomas, 1985.
40. Jacobson, A., and Lawhon, T. "Helping Children Manage Stress." *Dimensions* 11, no. 2 (1983): 8–10.
41. John, B., and Johns, M. "Stress Burns Out Kids Too." *Learning* 11 (1983): 48–49.
42. Kittleson, M.; Flasck, E.; and Ragon, B. "Reducing Hospital Stress Through a Health Education Field Experience." *Health Education* 17, no. 4 (1986): 16–17.
43. Kuczen, B. "Even Kids Suffer from Stress." *Early Years* 15 (1984): 26–27.
44. Langer, S. *The Psychology of Control*. Beverly Hills, Calif.: Sage Publications, 1983.
45. Laong, A. "Facts About Childhood Hyperactivity." *Children Today* 13, no. 4 (1984): 8–13.
46. Lawhon, T., and Krishman, B. "New Teacher: Avoiding Stress Overload." *Dimensions* 14, no. 2 (1986): 11–14.
47. Lazarus, R., and Folkman, S. *Stress: Appraisal and Coping*. New York:

Springer Publishing, 1984.

48. Lee. M. "Life Space: The Great Balancing Act." *Psychology Today* 20, no. 1 (1986): 48–57.

49. Long, S. "Mobile Lifestyles: Creating Change and Adaptation for Children and Adults." *Dimensions* 13, no. 2 (1985): 7–11.

50. _____. "The Single Parent Family: Concerns and Issues." *Delta Kappa Gamma Bulletin* 50 (1984): 49–56.

51. Longfellow, C., and Belle, D. "Stressful Environments and Their Impact on Childen." In *Mother-Child, Father-Child Relationships*, edited by J. H. Stevens and M. Matthews. Washington, D.C.: National Association for the Education of Young Children, 1978.

52. Lourie, R., and Schwarzbeck, C. "When Children Feel Helpless in the Face of Stress." *Childhood Education* 55 (1979): 134–40.

53. Lynn D. "Peer Helpers: Increasing Positive Student Involvement in Schools." *The School Counselor* 34, no. 1 (1986): 62–66.

54. Maier, S., and Laudenslager, M. "Stress and Health: Exploring the Links." *Psychology Today* 19, no. 8 (1985): 44–49.

55. Manning, M., and Manning, G. "The School's Assault on Childhood." *Childhood Education* 58 (1981): 84–87.

56. McGuire, D., and Ely, M. "Childhood Suicide." *Childhood Welfare* 63, no. 1 (1984): 17–26.

57. Meredith, K. "Strike-O-Graph: The Psychological Diet Chart." *Transactional Analysis Journal* 16, no. 3 (1986): 161-64.

58. Miller, M. *Childstress*. Garden City, N.Y.: Doubleday, 1982.

59. Montagu, A. "Friendship." *Child Care Information Exchange* 50 (1986): 25.

60. National Institute of Child Health. *Malnutrition, Learning, and Behavior*. Washington, D.C.: U.S. Government Printing Office, 1978. DHEW Publication No. 76-1036.

61. Nimnicht, G. "Back to Basics: More Tender Loving Care for Young Children." *Young Children* 36, no. 5 (1981): 4–11.

62. Oden, S., and Asher, S. "Coaching Children in Social Skills for Friendship Making." *Child Development* 48 (1977): 495–506.

63. Packard, V. *Our Endangered Children*. Boston: Little, Brown, 1983.

64. Pelletier, K. *Mind as Healer, Mind as Slayer*. New York: Delta Publishing, 1977.

65. Postman, N. *The Disappearance of Childhood*. New York: Delacorte Press, 1982.

66. Powell, A. "Being Unspecial in the Shopping Mall High School." *Phi Delta Kappan* 67, no. 4 (1985): 255–61.

67. Purkey, W., and Novak, J. *Inviting School Success: A Self-Concept Approach to Teaching and Learning*. Belmont, Calif.: Wadsworth Publishing, 1984.

68. Reed, S. "Stress: What Makes Kids Vulnerable?" *Instructor* 93 (1984): 28–31.

69. Rhiner, P. "Pressures on Today's Children." *PTA Today* 8 (1983): 4–8.

70. Rosenthal, P., and Rosenthal, S. "Suicide Among Preschoolers: Fact or

Fallacy." *Children Today* 12, no. 6 (1983): 21–24.

71. Rubin, Z. *Children's Friendships*. Cambridge, Mass.: Harvard University Press, 1980.

72. Santrock, J., and Yussen, S. *Children and Adolescents: A Developmental Perspective*. Dubuque, Iowa: W.C. Brown, 1984.

73. Schultz, E., and Heuchart, C. *Child Stress and the School Experience*. New York: Human Sciences Press, 1983.

74. Segal, J., and Segal, Z. "The Powerful World of Peer Relationships." *American Educator* 10, no. 2 (1986): 14–17.

75. Silvernail, D. *Developing Positive Student Self-Concept*. 2d ed. Washington, D.C.: National Education Association, 1985.

76. Suransky, V. *The Erosion of Childhood*. Chicago: The University of Chicago Press, 1982.

77. Swick, K. *A Proactive Approach to Discipline*. Washington, D.C.: National Education Association, 1985.

78. _____, and Hanley, P. *Stress and the Classroom Teacher*. 2d ed. Washington, D.C.: National Education Association, 1985.

79. Wallis, C. "Stress: Can We Cope?" *Time* (June 6, 1983): 48–54.

80. Weisner, M. "Childhood: An Endangered Concept." *Journal of Special Education* 19 (1983): 50–54.

81. Winn, M. "What Became of Childhood Innocence?" *New York Times Magazine* January 25, 1981.

82. Wolff, S. *Children Under Stress*. New York: Penguin Books, 1981.

83. Workman, B. "Dear Professor: This Is What I Want You to Know." *Phi Delta Kappan* 67, no. 9 (1986): 668–71.

84. Ziegenhagen, N. "A Curriculum for Caring." *Childhood Education* 59, no. 1 (1982): 2–7.

ADDITIONAL READINGS

Charles, C. M. *Elementary Classroom Management*. New York: Longman, 1983.

"Children Under Stress." *U.S. News and World Report*, October 27, 1986.

Fairchild, Thomas N. *Crisis Intervention Strategies for School-Based Helpers*. Springfield, Ill.: Charles C. Thomas, 1986.

Glasser, William. *Control Theory in the Classroom*. New York: Harper and Row, 1986.

Greenberg, Sheldon. *Stress and the Teaching Profession*. Baltimore: Paul H. Brookes, 1984.

Huth, Holly Young. *Centerplay: Focusing Your Child's Energy*. New York: Simon and Schuster, 1984.

Rekers, George. *Family Building*. Ventura, Calif.: Regal Books, 1985.

Swick, Kevin J. *Maintaining Productive Student Behavior*. Rev. ed. Washington, D.C.: National Education Association, 1981.

Swick, Kevin J. *Parents and Teachers as Discipline Shapers*. Washington, D.C.: National Education Association, 1985.

Swick, Kevin J., and Duff, Eleanor. *Parenting*. Washington, D.C.: National Education Association, 1979.

Swick, Kevin J., and Hanley, Patricia E. *Teacher Renewal: Revitalization of Classroom Teachers*. Washington, D.C.: National Education Association, 1983.

Winn, Marie. *Children Without Childhood*. New York: Pantheon Books, 1983.